LET GO OF THE FEAR

∞

POWERFUL STORIES & LESSONS
ON HOW TO LIVE A BOLD AND FEARLESS LIFE

BY MICHELLE HILLAERT

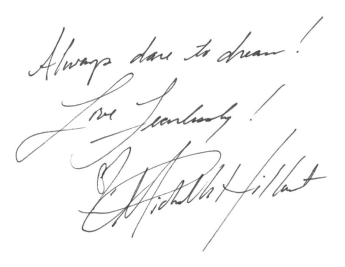

Always dare to dream!
Love Fearlessly!
Michelle Hillaert

Printed in the United States of America

700 E. Redlands Blvd, Suite U #293
Redlands, CA 92373

Cataloging-in-Publication data for this book is available from the Library of Congress

ISBN 978-0-9976032-0-0

Copies of this book are available at special discounts for bulk purchases in the U.S. by schools, non-profit organizations, and other government and private agencies. For more information, please contact the Special Markets Department, Full Circle Press at 700 E. Redlands Blvd, Ste U #293, Redlands, CA 92373 or at www.fullcirclepress.org.

Cover design and layout by Laura Marie.

This is a work of nonfiction. Personal events are portrayed to the best of the author's memory and the ideas are original, but have been influenced by a variety of readings, trainings, personal and professional development workshops, and other experiences that the author has encountered throughout the years. While all the stories in this book are based on true events and interviews that the author and publisher conducted with real women, some names and identifying details have been changed to protect the privacy of the people involved. The opinions expressed in the stories are those of the women interviewed and do not necessarily reflect the viewpoints of the author.

The information contained in this book is for informational purposes only and should not be used to replace the specialized training and professional judgment of a health care or mental health care professional. The reader should consult with his/her doctor in any matters relating to his/her health and should consult a physician or a trained mental health professional before making any decision regarding treatment of self or others. This book is not meant to be used, nor should it be used, to diagnose or treat any medical condition. It is sold with the understanding that neither the author nor publisher are engaged to render any type of medical, psychological, or other professional advice. Neither the publisher nor the author shall be held liable for any physical, psychological, emotional, financial, or commercial damages, including, but not limited to, special, incidental, consequential, or other damage.

LET GO OF THE FEAR

∞

POWERFUL STORIES & LESSONS
ON HOW TO LIVE A BOLD AND FEARLESS LIFE

DEDICATION

To my God, who loves all, forgives all, and casts out the fear.

For my husband, Trent. You are my hero, my greatest gift, and proof that God cherishes me. It is your beautiful gift of love that has patiently broken down the walls of my heart. You show me every day that I am lovable and that I am worthy. It is because of you that I can let go of the fear. I love you forever and for always.

For my children - Joseph, Brigette, Nichole, Margarette, Jacqueline and Augustine - my mini-mes, my heroes. You are forever etched in my heart, my DNA. I love you with all that I am.

CONTENTS

∞

When a resolute young fellow steps up to the great bully, the world, and takes him boldly by the beard, he is often surprised to find it comes off in his hand, and that it was only tied on to scare away the timid adventurers.

– Ralph Waldo Emerson

LETTER TO THE READER

Dear Reader,

This book is my gift to you. A gift that says it's *okay* if you feel afraid. A gift that says you're not alone in that fear. A gift that says I've been on this journey too and that I know that it's possible to move through and beyond our fears. This book is also a message of hope that says even though we may feel fear, and even though we might feel like we're stuck, there is a way out.

Because we know ourselves most intimately – our insecurities, our hurts, our failures – we're often so blinded by what's holding us back that we can't see the beauty that lies within. We're fighting our inner voices that sometimes whisper and other times shout, "You're not good enough. You're not perfect. You're a failure." Or even worse, "You're completely unlovable."

These fears – and they're all fears – can stop us from living, dreaming and believing in ourselves. It's often hard to see beyond them, but what we'll learn as we begin to let go of our fear is that yes, we *are* lovable and we *are* worthy. And yes, we *can* live bold and fearless lives.

So here I am, reaching out to you and saying, "Hey! I've been there. I'm still walking this path, and I've found a way to keep walking and have linked arms with other women who have too! Take hold of my hand and let's do this together."

Let's put on some hot water for tea or make a fresh pot of joe, pour it into our favorite cup, and start sipping on the steamy goodness as we learn to quiet those inner voices that tell us "I can't" and reawaken our God-given ability to dream. Because you, my friend, are a captivating soul. You are fearfully and wonderfully made. And my sister, you were made for *more*!

With all my love,

Michelle

PREFACE

Their story, yours, mine – it's what we all carry with us on this trip we take, and we owe it to each other to respect our stories and learn from them.

– William Carlos Williams

The process of writing this book started with filtering through some of my own ideas about what it means to name, claim and overcome fear. From there, I wrote through concepts that I've been exploring for the past few years in my work coaching and mentoring women. Once I had a solid framework, I started processing all of my own stories and experiences surrounding fear. Although many of my own fear stories do not appear in the pages that follow, writing and talking about them did help me come to a place where I was equipped to write the book you're now reading.

I drew from my own experience when developing a framework on fear because I wanted the message to come from a woman who had lived and sorted through all this personally, not from an expert on the topic of fear, which I'm not. What's being shared here and the stories that unfold in this book – none of it is new. These stories have been told in other voices, perhaps even in your own.

As I delved deeper into the writing process, I started to reach out to women in my own circle and was surprised at how many of them had experienced fear in some compelling ways. Hearing these women's stories was a great reminder of how much we can learn from taking the time to really *listen* to those around us, and how little we tend to do this in our daily lives. The pain and triumphs that some of my friends shared taught me that we often don't know what another woman holds in her heart – and the fears she carries with her and has overcome – until we ask, and then listen.

The stories you will read throughout this book are the real life experiences of women who have faced and overcome fear in some complex and challenging ways. These stories illustrate how fear can keep us from growing until we learn how to truly name, claim and overcome it in our own lives.

It was important that I included stories from women who teach us all – through both their courage and vulnerability – how fear shows up every day and what it takes to live beyond fear. As I started to interview the women, it became clear that although there were some common threads in what they shared, there was also a lot of variety. For example, some women defined fear as a choice and others defined it as an involuntary response to a real event. Some women spoke about fear being a positive force of change in their lives and others spoke about it being something to avoid at all costs. Many women talked about how childhood fears continue to show up in their lives today, whereas other women were able to distinctly separate their childhood fears from those they struggle with in adulthood.

Many women spoke about the role that faith has personally played in their own fear journeys. So whether or not some of these stories speak the same faith language as our own, my hope is that we can still connect with the hearts of the women sharing their stories, because in the end, that's what we are – women with hearts that have been somehow affected by fear.

What also came to light during the interviews is that no matter how much we've grappled with fear, it's not something that's always easy to talk about. There were a lot of tears shed during the interviewing and writing phases of this book. There were some times when the women were reluctant to talk about fear, and other times when they kept talking long after the interviews ended.

Talking, writing and reading about fear isn't necessarily fun, it definitely isn't pretty, and it isn't always able to be tucked neatly into a vision of the world that makes sense. If I've learned anything from my own journey through fear and from listening to the stories of all the women interviewed, it's that even those of us who live the most fearless lives still have fear and still struggle with this fear in ways both large and small. And yet we've learned to do incredibly bold and brave and beautiful things *in spite of* that fear. At the end of the day, it's this type of fearlessness that I want for all of us. Because it's not just life changing, it's life transforming. It doesn't just change *some* things. It changes *everything*.

So my hope is that you'll read these women's stories in a way that not only makes you think about how you process your own fear, but also inspires you to face some of these fears head on and reflect deeply on your own purpose and vision for your life. This is a book about fear, of course, but it's also about life and courage and hope and what it takes to step out in faith and inspire others to do the same.

Even though each of us has to walk our own paths and follow our own truths, we don't have to go the journey alone. Through the entire process of writing this book, I've thought of you, dear reader, walking right beside me through it all. This book belongs to all of us.

THE DREAM DARE

∞

*The biggest adventure you can ever take
is to live the life of your dreams.*

– Oprah Winfrey

Do you dare to dream – I mean, *really* dream? If you were to take out all the "I can'ts," "What ifs," and "If onlys," and really allow yourself to dream, what would you do? Where would you go? Who would you become? Have you even *thought* about it?

Do it right now. I dare you. Close your eyes and DREAM. If you could do *anything*, or become *anyone*, what would you do and who would you become? Where would you live? How would you spend your days? What contributions would you make to the world? How would you shape your legacy?

Now, think about yourself actually *living* the life of your dreams. How do you feel now?   Thrilled? Intimidated? Breathless? Excited? Scared?

As children, most of us have this amazing ability to dream. Our imaginations run wild and the world is at our doorstep. But somewhere between the age of make-believe and adulthood, many of us lose the ability to believe that we can do whatever it is we *want* to do and be whomever it is we *want* to be. We get lost in a world we create for ourselves that is safe and comfortable. We go about our lives following a predictable routine and staying in the same patterns, often so busy that we can hardly think to the next day, much less to the next month, year or years. But then one day, a tiny seed is planted and starts to grow. We start to wonder, "Maybe there is something more out there for me. Maybe I *can* follow my dream." Our dream builds and builds until we can't hold it in any longer. So we test it out and start taking steps forward, inching our way toward the edge of our safety zone.

As we get closer to this boundary, our chest tightens, we find it hard to breathe, and we begin to panic as we stand there unable to move. What's out there? What if I get lost? What if I fail? What if? What if? What if...?

It's dark. It's cold. It's FEAR.

Fear is sometimes hard to recognize, let alone acknowledge, because even though we live in a world filled with fear, we don't often speak openly about it. Maybe it's because as adults we feel we're not *supposed* to be afraid. Maybe it's because we're scared that if we do talk about fear, it will suddenly become real. And maybe we feel that if we talk about our fears openly, we'll be faced with the challenge to *change* – change ourselves, change our circumstances, change our mindsets. And let's face it, change is often scary in and of itself, which leaves us right back where we started – unable to even name our fears, let alone do anything to claim and overcome them.

Although this book focuses primarily on how fear affects us personally, as with many areas of life, much of what we do and experience not only affects our own lives, but also impacts our families and communities. This ripple effect explains why a woman who marries an abusive husband is more likely to have a daughter who grows up and marries an abusive man like her own father. Or why a daughter who grows up watching her mom eat unhealthy food is more likely to struggle with her own weight and a host of health-related illnesses as an adult. But it's also why the daughter of a marathon runner grows up to become not only a runner herself, but also a coach who helps others get healthy. Or why the daughter of a successful entrepreneur starts her own business and sets herself up for a lifetime of success.

Why would having the ability to dream be any different? We often learn our limitations and our abilities from our parents and other role models. What *can* they do? What *can't* they do? The best gift I received from my own mom, who graduated with her nursing license at the age of 66, was knowing that I could tackle anything that came my way. If I *really* wanted to do or learn something new, I had no doubt that I could do it. It's this "I can" mindset that has pushed me and has allowed me to tackle things in life, including my own healing, with such vigor. I *can* sew. I *can* play piano. I *can* splice electrical cords. I *can* write a book. *I can. I can. I can.* And I know that I *can* because I never heard my mom say "I can't."

Whether we're married or single and have our own children or not, most of us have young people in our lives who learn from the example we set. When we don't follow *our* dreams, they learn from this. They listen to our words and they *watch* our actions. They pay attention to everything, including how we push ourselves outside of our comfort zones or how we allow our fears to keep us where we know we're safe. So having the ability to dream isn't just about us, it's also so much bigger than that.

We have this incredible opportunity to break the cycle of fear and begin a new legacy with our own children and other young people we influence. A legacy where we boldly try new things. Where we have the courage to dream big and act on these dreams. And yes, where we can even learn to let go of our fear along the way.

∞

We begin this journey together in Part I by taking a good look at what fear is, why we fear and how we personally define both fear and fearlessness. We sort through both real and perceived fear in order to discern which fears keep us safe and which ones hold us back and then discuss three facets of fear that affect why, how and when we fear. We then look at the deep roots of our fear so we can understand why we fear to begin with, how our childhoods affect our fear today, and how and why fear shows up for so many of us in our daily lives. We learn why we need to be able to understand our root fears and claim them before we can even begin the work to overcome them.

In Part II we walk through specific strategies we can use to overcome fear. First, we get clear on our WHY and figure out what will motivate us through the times when things get tough and we just want to give up. Next, we dive into the importance of developing a more positive mindset. Then we look at why forgiveness plays such an important role in letting go of our fear. We end with learning how to act in spite of our fears, live freely, and follow our dreams.

Now I can't promise that this journey through fear will be easy, but I can promise it *will* be worth it. When we commit ourselves wholeheartedly to working through our fears and open our hearts enough to learn from the women who so honestly share their stories with us, then we begin to recognize our own fears more clearly and gain the perspective and tools we need to name them, claim them, and then truly overcome them.

So here is my challenge to you, my friend. I *dare* you to take this journey. I *dare* you to allow yourself to be vulnerable enough to let down your walls and truly face your fears. I *dare* you to see the value, beauty and worthiness in *you*. I dare you be bold, to be strong, to be fearless, and to allow yourself to *dream*.

PART I

NAMING AND CLAIMING IT

∞

The beginning of wisdom is to
call things by their right names.

– Confucius

CHAPTER

1

THE F WORD:
DEFINING FEAR & FEARLESSNESS

∞

*Nothing in life is to be feared, it is only to
be understood. Now is the time to understand
more, so that we may fear less.*

– Marie Curie

Fear. Every day we are faced with fears. Some are so obvious that we can't possibly miss them. Others are so hidden that we have no clue they're there and we don't even see how they drive our everyday decisions.

To put it bluntly, if we're not moving forward – if there's something that's holding us back from pursuing what we really want or from breaking down those walls that we've built so strongly around our hearts – that something is probably fear. And as we'll see in the stories throughout the book, fear is such a complex subject in part because it shows up and affects us in so many different ways.

When we figure out what fear really is and what role it plays in our lives, we can then look within and name the fears that stop us from things such as loving completely, trying new things, or pursuing our dreams.

You see, we might *feel* stuck, but we're not actually stuck. We simply struggle with knowing how to navigate through it all. And to be honest, we often don't even understand *what* we're trying to navigate through in the first place.

Our first story comes from a woman who had some very valid reasons early in life to let her fears define her and hold her back from truly living. When Tara's doctor spoke fear over her at the age of eight by naming her "I can't do its," fear entered her life in a way that it might not have otherwise. For many years, fear constantly told her "You can't do it" every time she met someone new or wanted to walk more than a mile. Tara's story teaches us that when we have a clear understanding of what our fears are and where they come from, we can not only name them, but also work through them with determination and focus.

∞

I DON'T THINK HE KNEW THAT THE FEAR HE PLANTED IN ME ON THAT SINGLE DAY WOULD FOREVER BE IN THE BACK OF MY MIND. FROM THEN ON, WHEN FACED WITH A CHALLENGE MY FIRST THOUGHT WOULD BE "I CAN'T DO IT!" EVEN THOUGH MY FAITH WAS SAYING, "YES, YOU CAN."

- TARA

Tara is a 37-year-old motivational speaker, author, educator, change agent, mother and wife. Her belief is that your purpose will impact others and this belief continues to enable her to help people move into their destinies.

When we're born, we have two instincts inside of us - fear and faith. Fear doesn't *want* you to fulfill your purpose, but faith allows you to believe you can do anything. You see, I was born without a socket in my left hip - a condition called developmental dysplasia. My parents took me to a doctor when I was eight years old and I remember sitting in that office listening to the doctor describe to my parents what *would* and *wouldn't* happen in my life as I grew up. He spoke to my parents, not realizing that he was also speaking over my life. I remember he said that I wouldn't be able to walk more than a mile, have kids, or participate in the activities I loved like dancing and cheerleading. His words hit me hard.

We have to be so careful how we speak over the lives of others, because this doctor planted fear in me when he said I would never be able to have kids. He instilled this fear that I would never be fulfilled as a mom and that I'd never be able to participate in dance or sports or walk more than a mile. From then on, when faced with a challenge my first thought would be, "I can't do it!" even though my faith was saying, "Yes, you can."

So from the age of eight, that doctor's words turned into fear and then the fear turned into all the "I can'ts" in my life. Even when I started to date, I would tell guys right away that I could never have kids. My initial response to so much in my life was to say what I couldn't do.

It took years upon years of speaking positive affirmations into my life and knowing that God had a bigger plan to get me to the place I am today. I had to battle a lot of low self esteem. I had to tell myself, "You *can* do this. You *can* walk more than a mile. You *can* have kids." Because with fear, we have to make sure that every time we're hit with an "I can't" that we tell *ourselves* what we *can* do – what we've been destined and called to do.

I have two daughters now, and my hope is that everything I do as an entrepreneur and the way I approach my life and my destiny shows them that no one should ever tell them what they can or cannot do. I've never said that I'm afraid in front of my daughters, but I hope that if they do see that I'm a little scared, they'll also see that this fear won't ever stop me from doing what I know I need to do. When they see Mommy, they see that Mommy is a hustler. They see that Mommy doesn't just talk, she gets it done. She manifests big things in her life, and she gets out there. They may say, "Mommy was a little afraid," but they will also believe that "Mommy *will* do it because the calling in her life is bigger than her fears." That's my hope.

If I had given in to all the fear that was spoken over my life at a young age, I wouldn't be living the life I am today. I truly believe that if we conquer fear we can boldly walk into our destinies, because fear is the enemy saying, "Don't do that." Fear keeps us hostage and doesn't allow us to positively impact the lives of others. Fear is saying, "I don't want you to do what you were called to do, because if you do that you defeat me." Fear doesn't allow us to win. The beauty of it all is that when we decide to operate outside of fear, we *do* win.

∞

Having lived with fear from the time she was eight years old, Tara had to actively navigate through her fears for many years before she truly learned how to live fearlessly. You see, to be fearless doesn't mean we don't have fear. It means that we're able to walk forward with and through our fears. It means that sometimes we embrace our fears and sometimes we tell them where to go because we're able to call them out for what they *really* are. And it means that as long as our dreams are bigger than our fears, then we know that we have no choice but to overcome them. Our fears are not gone, but they no longer have control over who we are or what we do. Being fearless means that we've learned to act in spite of fear, dream in spite of fear, and *live* – truly live – in spite of fear.

That being said, it's important that we define both fear and fearlessness for *ourselves* because *how* we deal with fear is often directly connected with how we define it. What I saw clearly in my interviews is that very often the way a woman defines fearlessness is directly connected to both her definition of fear and what she's experienced in her own life.

In this next story, we get a glimpse into the complexity of fear and the many ways it can impact us. Audrey clearly names what both fear and fearlessness mean to her and how they're connected to the experiences she's had in life as both a mom and a biology professor.

∞

THE THINGS WE HAVE TO WORK THROUGH IN LIFE ARE NOT MOUNTAINS, THEY'RE CHALLENGES. THEY'RE DARES. THEY DARE YOU TO SURVIVE THIS AND DO IT WELL. DON'T FALL, CLIMB.

- AUDREY

Audrey is a 47-year-old mom of three who has been married for 25 years. She's a biology professor and has two sons who have served in the military. In her spare time, Audrey loves to crochet and volunteer at her church.

I know from what I experienced as a child that the circumstances of your youth *do* make you who you are when you're older. But we can't live as victims in our heads, letting other people or all the rotten things that have happened in our lives hold us captive. You know that saying, "What doesn't kill you makes you stronger?" That's true. There will always be those people who are going to hurt our feelings and think we're weird. We just need to be like, "I'm good." They're either going to love us as we are - or not. This gives us an opportunity to grow in the ways we need to most.

Understanding fear is also a matter of understanding the way our brains work. Anxiety and fear are hardwired and some people have more tendencies to be anxious and fearful genetically. When we stop and realize that the very nature of fear is a biochemical thing, it can help calm us down. We can go to a doctor if we need to. We can deal with our physical anxiety by exercising, talking to someone, or realizing that maybe we're just fine.

My biggest fear is losing my kids. People lose kids all the time, so it's really not a far-fetched fear. I beg God not to take them. My kids are my everything. I'm not that mom who lives vicariously through her kids. They are beautiful creations of the Lord and they are His, but I want them to live good, happy, healthy lives and to spread happiness in this ugly world.

Twice with one of my sons and once with one of my daughters, we thought they were dead. I'll never forget the day when we heard that a 17-year-old boy and his girlfriend had drowned at a lake. People had seen my son swimming in that lake with his girlfriend shortly before the drowning was reported, and the next thing we knew we heard of the tragedy and couldn't reach him. The whole neighborhood was looking for him and it was really terrifying. Yet even then, I still had to move through my fear and tell myself to do what I was supposed to do. That's the only level of fear that's worth worrying about to me. I still feel bad that I was relieved to find it wasn't my son who drowned. It was an awful day.

Both my boys went to Iraq and Afghanistan. When my older son left I didn't really believe he was gone – in my mind he was going to be home every weekend, even though that wasn't true. And of course my husband kept telling me that everything was fine. When my son went to Iraq, that was the first time I was scared. I cried and worried, but was not paralyzed. After he got back, I saw what war had done to him. So after that, every military experience was terror.

When my younger son went away to boot camp, I finally understood. I knew that he was really leaving and that life would never be the same. I was probably more paralyzed with fear during that time than I've ever been in my life, because I was afraid he was going to do something stupid and have his head cut off. He is a different kid – he pushes boundaries and I feared that could have been the end of him.

I was beside myself for six months and was really losing it. I was just not okay. One day my older daughter, who was a teenager at the time, sat down on my bed when I was crying and told me, "You know when you act like this, Mom, it makes us feel like we're not as important to you as he is, and we're still here and my brother's going to be okay. And even if he's not, you can't live your life in fear." It took her saying "I'm still here, Mom" to wake me up. Sometimes fear can be so destructive if you don't snap out of it. Luckily, I had my daughter to help me do that.

We will always have fear. You can be faithful and love the Lord, but the truth is fear is a part of life. Not all fear is bad, though. Some fear is good. God gave us fear to help us survive. We *should* be afraid of what drugs will do to our lives. I want my kids to be afraid of me finding out that they've been at a party drinking. You should also be afraid of God. God is a loving God and wants good things for us, but he also says, "Hear Me!"

Fear is a paralyzer. You don't know how you will take a step, but you just do. The things we have to work through in life are not mountains, they're challenges. They're dares. They *dare* you to survive this and do it well. Don't fall, climb.

So how do we deal with fear? How do we get to be strong? I am strong because of Jesus, and if you want to share my story, you can only do it if you give Him top billing. If I'm going to change someone's life, it's because of Him. The opposite of fear is love, and in the end, when I die, what I want people to remember about me is "She loved and she loved with her whole heart."

∞

Audrey's story of fear shows the complexity of fear and why it's so important to understand not only what fear is, but how and why it shows up in our lives. Naming fear is more than just defining it. It's about understanding what we fear, why we fear and when we fear. It's recognizing how our fear from the past affects our fear.

Audrey's story of fear shows the complexity of fear and why it's so important to understand not only what fear is, but how and why it shows up in our lives. Naming fear is more than just defining it. It's about understanding what we fear, why we fear and when we fear. It's recognizing how our fear from the past affects our fear in the future and knowing why sometimes we can experience fear and be in danger, and yet other times experience fear and be quite safe.

Why We Fear

So let's take the first step on this journey and look at fear itself to answer the most obvious questions – What is fear anyway and why do we *feel* fear?

Simply put, fear is commonly defined as "an unpleasant belief that someone or something is dangerous, likely to cause pain, or a threat."

The key word here is "belief." We feel fear because we *believe* we're in some sort of danger. That's it. And we were actually created to feel this fear. Just as a porcupine stands its quills on end to protect itself when it senses danger, we too were created to have a physical reaction when we sense that we are not safe.

So we were *born* to feel that chilling sensation creep up our spine. We were created to feel that vise grip on our chest and that lump in our throat, which begs the question of why. Why would we be *created* to feel something that can easily stop us from experiencing a happy and fulfilled life?

We know that waiting on the other side of every fear is freedom. Right? Although that may *seem* right at first, it's not necessarily always true. We were created to both feel fear and sense danger in order to help keep us safe. If we stop to think about it, virtually every animal has some sort of built-in defense mechanism for protection – blending into the background, sporting a hard shell to protect the body, having an incredible ability to take off and run. Why would we be any different?

We're not. When we sense danger, our fear sends out warning signals through our body that shout, "You're not safe! Protect yourself! *Run*!"

So yes, sometimes fear can be good or even necessary for survival. It keeps us from crossing a busy road without looking both ways or from touching a hot burner on the stove. Fear can help us navigate our days safely and prevent us from getting hurt. So again, to say that on the other side of every fear is freedom doesn't always make sense. Without a natural inborn sense of fear helping us maneuver through life, we would very likely find ourselves in dangerous situations and even struggle to survive.

Now that we know *why* we were created to fear, we need to take a deeper look at the fears that don't protect us and that aren't directly connected with physical danger. For instance, if we're on a country road and there are no cars for miles around, but we're afraid to cross for fear of getting hit, we might *feel* afraid even though in all reality we're quite safe. The same could be said of being afraid to touch a stove that's not on. Because we've been burned before, we *feel* fear regardless of the fact that we're actually not in danger.

Taking it to a deeper level, maybe it's not the stove we're afraid of being burned by, but the fear of something that's hurt us in the past. These fears can stop us from letting people into our hearts. They can stop us from dreaming and can drive our inner voices to shout, "I can't!" Perhaps these fears leave us feeling that we're unworthy of love or achieving a dream, and we feel trapped and unsure of how to move forward, or if it's even possible.

These voices we hear – the ones that stop us from trying new things or pursuing our dreams – *these* are the fears we are naming here. Because even though we might show the world that we're made of steel and even sometimes lead people to think we're a bit like Wonder Woman, in all reality we're often terrified on the inside. And because of our own complex fear stories, we often find that in order to prevent fear from taking over and running our lives, we become numb. We accept things we shouldn't and convince ourselves that we're just fine. That our lives are okay as they are. That fear is something that we're just going to have to live with.

We Deserve to Thrive

There is so much more for us than surviving and living in spite of whatever fears hold us back, though. We can *thrive* in life. But to do this, we *have* to address our fears head-on. This means possibly opening up doors that we'd rather leave closed or showing the world that the perfect exteriors we often display might have some serious cracks in them.

You see, we were created to succeed and to dream. But in order to get out of our own way so we can move forward, we first have to go back and name the fears that build those thick and often impenetrable walls around our hearts, the fears that tell us we're not worthy of success, the fears that say "I can't."

We need to be able to clearly name our *root* fears – those deeply held fears that drive all of our other fears – in order to get unstuck and pursue our dreams.

Real versus Perceived Fear

Isn't it interesting how we can be excited to go to an amusement park and intentionally hop on a roller coaster, strap ourselves in, and then scream in excited horror as we take the deep dives and fast turns? And yet, if we're in a car driving down a mountain and the brakes suddenly give out, even though we may be experiencing similar dives and turns, we are gripped with fear and barely able to breathe.

As we see in this example, all fear is not created equal and there are many different facets of fear. Our fears might be similar in description, yet very different in how they affect us. Two types of fear – real fear and perceived fear – can both excite us, send chills down our spines, and leave us feeling very much afraid.

And yet for all their similarities, these two fears differ in the dangers they present to our safety. It's important to look at the difference between real and perceived fear so we can recognize where the boundaries of our comfort zones are and learn when and how to use fear as a valid warning sign of danger and when and how to work through our fear.

Real Fear

Imagine you're crossing the street and a car swerves around you, nearly knocking you to the ground. The fear you feel in the moment when all you hear is the screeching of car tires so close to you is *real*. The physical danger is present, you know you could be seriously injured or even killed, and every part of your body is reacting to the fear you feel.

Sometimes when we're faced with scary and traumatic situations, even if we're in real danger, our reactions can be complex. We might *think* we'd be feeling real fear, but when something traumatic happens, we might not actually feel fear in the moment. This is what we'll see in the next story with Cassidy. Cassidy's life-changing experience illustrates the complicated nature of how real fear does, and does not, show up in times of tragedy. It also shows how our entire outlook on fear can change in the aftermath of something traumatic.

∞

I FEEL LIKE FEAR SHOWS UP NOW IN EVERYTHING IN MY LIFE — IN MY PERSONAL LIFE, IN MY INTERACTIONS WITH OTHER PEOPLE, AND ESPECIALLY WITH MAKING CHOICES TO OPEN UP TO A FRIEND OR TO SOMEONE ROMANTICALLY. AND IT SHOWS UP IN MY RECREATIONAL ACTIVITIES WHEN I'M TAKING ON HARD CHALLENGES.

- CASSIDY

Cassidy is a single, 31-year-old outdoor educator and rock climber who grew up in Southern California. She spends a good part of the year working at an Antarctica research station.

I spend a lot of time doing things that many women probably consider extreme and scary. Although it might seem like I'm pretty fearless, that's not necessarily true. Both professionally and recreationally I've always tried to control a lot. Part of my fear is when I don't have control of things. So when I do things that may seem riskier, like trying a hard climbing route, I take steps to control the situation and make sure that I'm as prepared and safe as possible.

I faced real fear a few years ago on a remote camping trip to Colorado with my then-boyfriend, Jacob, who was also an experienced outdoorsman. I think it's important for people to know that when you're rock climbing or on a trip like this with someone, you really make decisions together. That day, we took a canoe out on a windy alpine lake. I knew we were heading out in rougher conditions and that Jacob wasn't a strong swimmer. Even though I questioned whether we should take the canoe out that day, in a partnership you can't over impose your fear too much over someone else. So we went out in spite of my reservations, and it wasn't long before the winter conditions worsened and we recognized that we needed to get to shore as quickly as possible.

By that time, there were extraordinary external forces - the high winds and the waves and the freezing water - so I couldn't even connect with how bad things were for both of us. In times of trial it's so much better to focus on a way out of the immediate danger and push through than it is to focus on the negative. I could have been like, "Oh, it's cold and that's bad and I hate being wet," but instead my mind was reeling with, "It's cold. Let's get out of this water as quickly as possible and get hot water bottles and move forward."

Things got worse quickly. Within seconds, I could barely move my hands, which made me think, "Yep, that's a bad sign." I knew that I was going to have to test my physical ability, and was making decisions based off of that. It was surreal. I don't know if fear is the right way to put it - but take all the fear you've ever had in your life and then have a situation happen where every possible fear is there.

In the moment, I don't even know if what I was feeling was fear because I wasn't even quite sure what was happening. All I knew was that Jacob was in trouble and I was in trouble. I'm sure fear was a part of the process, but it was almost like fear was a third person running in my head making things happen. And I was just pushing myself to the limit to do whatever I could in that moment. It was like I was in a military drill or something.

To me, the most horrible thing in the world is watching a person you love die in front of you, and that's what happened that day. I was running on something bigger than thinking Jacob had just passed away. It was so traumatic, but I was still in physical danger myself and had to keep making one decision after another. I had to keep pushing myself. I knew the level at which I was operating wasn't sustainable. It's all pretty incomprehensible to some extent, because the whole time I was still thinking "How can I possibly make this situation better for him and for me?" That's where it felt like I almost had a dual personality. I was thinking, "Well, if I can get to this level, maybe I can..." But my mind was like, "Nope, you can't do that. Now is the time to get help because you won't make it out alive if you don't."

I was able to pull myself onto shore as frostbite was rapidly setting in, and I kept thinking, "I have to go back into the water" because I knew Jacob was still out there. But then I was like, "Nope, I can't do that. If I go back in, I won't make it back out."

I knew I needed to go get help, which meant that I somehow had to climb up the cliffs that surrounded the lake. I then had to hike through the snow for miles to find a group of campers that we had passed by earlier that day. By the time I got to them, the frostbite on my feet was bad and I was in a state of complete shock. I had pushed my body to its limit and once I was able to be in the care of others, my body just shut down.

It was a split-second decision to go get help, which is the reason I'm alive today. If I had let my emotions and fear control me, I would have been consumed by them and would not have made it out alive.

I've already experienced my deepest fear - losing my life partner. Now my kneejerk reaction is to be alone because it's hard to think somebody else will ever represent the same thing to me as Jacob does. So much in my life after the accident is about following through and honoring what our goals were and what we wanted to do together. That's really my drive. But it also makes me wonder if I'm going to be brave enough to be on my own for the rest of my life and to have that be enough. I know it doesn't have to be that way, but that's where I am today.

Because of the accident, I'm now most afraid of what I can't predict or control. For example, when I'm working outside at the fuel station in Antarctica and the weather changes - that's a variable I can't control and my initial reaction is fear.

I think I've gotten better at recognizing real fear, though. So if I'm afraid of an unknown that I can't control, I just ask myself whether my fear is a legitimate reason for not doing something. I ask, "What is the worst thing that can actually happen if I do this?" and sometimes that answer may be bad. It may be scary. But when it comes to making decisions and being able to separate out the fears, then I know if the fear is of my own creation then I just have to move through it.

I get to the other side of fear by spending a lot of time being reflective. When I'm attentive to what's going on in my mind, I can feel what I'm supposed to do. And this makes me less afraid. I might not know intellectually whether something is right, but I do know what's right for my soul. I know emotionally and spiritually what I should do.

This isn't to say that I'm fearless. I feel like fear shows up now in everything in my life – in my personal life, in my interactions with other people, and especially in making choices to open up to a friend or to someone romantically. And it shows up in my recreational activities when I'm taking on hard challenges. The most prominent way I've faced fear is in the work I've decided to do in Antarctica. I've made some difficult choices where the fear was overwhelming, but somehow I've been able to push through and not give in to the fear.

One of the things I now believe about fear is that people need to face things more head on, because discomfort is something we've forgotten how to deal with. It's okay to be in a place that's uncomfortable, especially for women, because we're so often afraid to let ourselves explore the next steps in life when things aren't a hundred percent guaranteed. We need to face fear, ask the right questions of it, and then push through it. Step out of it.

∞

Cassidy's fear in the moment of losing her boyfriend was so complex that she doesn't even know if she can call it by that name. But in the aftermath of this tragedy, she had to learn how to take a step back and look at her fear in order to determine if it's real fear, warning of danger ahead, or perceived fear through which she can proceed with caution.

There are so many situations – both tragic and not – in which real fear *does* take a front-row seat. We might feel real fear when we're in a school full of children, hear a loud *bang*, and don't know if something big fell or if the school's security has been breached and we need to silently gather the children and hide. And we might feel real fear when we watch someone we love go out into battle, not knowing if we'll ever see him or her again.

Taking a good look at real fear, it becomes rather clear that it often manifests when there is a major unknown in our lives. We might feel real fear when we go into situations where safety is taken out of the equation and we're left with a question mark, a great big unknown hanging in the balance.

Sometimes we experience this real fear in one tragic moment, but other times it's a longer, more drawn-out fear wrapped up in a future full of the unknown. In our next story, we'll see how Jeanne faced real fear when she was diagnosed with cancer while pregnant. For Jeanne, it was the strength she found in her faith and trust in God's plan for her life that helped pull her through.

∞

I REMEMBER STANDING THERE IN THE BATHROOM AT THE DOCTOR'S OFFICE AND JUST FEELING GOD TELLING ME THAT EVERYTHING WAS GOING TO BE OKAY.

- JEANNE

Jeanne is a 45-year-old mother who was diagnosed with breast cancer when she was in the second trimester of her pregnancy with her youngest child.

I went to the gynecologist for a routine check-up and they thought they felt a lump, so they referred me to a specialist. I went in for my first visit and was nervous and a little scared. I remember standing there in the bathroom at the doctor's office and just feeling God telling me that everything was going to be okay.

I did well at the beginning of chemotherapy. I was tired, but I think that's how most people feel. Before every treatment I would go to the priest and get a blessing, which helped calm all those real fears surrounding what I was going through. During my six rounds of chemo, I sat there with chemo drugs going into my body, knowing I had to stay focused on my baby's health. I knew that chemo reduces amniotic fluid and I knew that if my level got too low they would have to take my baby right away. So this fear was always in the back of my mind, but I just kept reminding myself of how God had made it clear to me that He wasn't done with me yet. And I knew I had a lot of people praying for both me and the baby.

I remember pulling hair out with my brush early on in my first round of treatment. I didn't think it would start falling out that fast. I was in shock. Then there was one time late in my pregnancy when I was having stomach pain. Although I knew it was from the chemo, I was still so afraid because I was carrying a child. In the end, everything checked out fine.

When it was time for my daughter to be born, I was scared. I was worried about the effects the chemo may have had on her while in utero and I prayed for God to help my beautiful baby girl to be healthy. They checked my baby after she was born, she was fine, and I was so relieved and grateful for all the prayers that had gotten me through.

I know I shouldn't be crying now that it's all over and everything's okay, but honestly it's a real struggle to hold back the tears just thinking about the fact that cancer could have killed me. You try to move beyond it, but its impact on your life doesn't go away. For me, fear is when you don't know what is coming next or if you're going to be able to handle it. I believe that facing those fears in the midst of what you're going through is what makes you fearless, and I don't believe this can be done without God.

∾

Jeanne shares that the way she was able to work through her very real fear was by finding strength in her faith in God and trusting that it would all be okay. She also learned from her experience that life is short and when we go through a scary time, fear often leaves scars on our hearts and souls. Like in the aftermath of a storm, we're often left sorting through our emotions and fears long after the immediate danger is gone.

Perceived Fear

Not all fear is tragic, though, and sometimes we even welcome the thrill that accompanies feeling afraid. Many of us love to experience the adrenaline rush that comes when we *feel* fear. We live in a world where often each day seems to mirror the next. We sometimes get tired of the mundane and simply long to feel *something*. So what do we do? We seek out the thrill that accompanies fear, without actually putting ourselves into real danger. In other words, we look for ways to experience the *symptoms* of fear without having to suffer the *consequences* of fear. Naming this type of fear as perceived fear can help us begin to understand the direct connection between fear and safety and how that affects our ability to let go of our fear.

We experience perceived fear through thrill-seeking adventures like skydiving, bungee jumping, roller coasters and haunted houses. We also might seek out thrills we *perceive* as safer – whether they actually are or not – like riding a motorcycle, galloping wildly on a horse, or driving fast on a winding road.

Imagine that you're about to go skydiving. You're on the plane, preparing to jump, and are so afraid that the fear practically stops you in your tracks. Eventually, though, you do jump. You're terrified, but as you're falling you start to feel the thrill, the adrenaline rush, and your excitement overtakes your fear. You're experiencing the adventure. You *feel* free. As we'll read in the story below, this is how Janet felt when she went skydiving at the age of 69.

∞

LOOKING BACK, I HOPE EVERYONE DECIDES TO MAKE A BIG LEAP, IN SPITE OF THEIR FEAR, AT LEAST ONCE IN THEIR LIFETIME.

-JANET

Janet is a 72-year-old adventurous mother and grandmother who admits that she is game to try anything.

My son had to skydive for his Navy Seal training a few years ago, and it sounded so exciting that I decided to follow suit. Initially, I wasn't nervous or afraid of the jump. I was excited about finally realizing one of my bucket list dreams. My only moment of fear came when I had to stick my feet out the open door of the plane at 9,000 feet. At that moment, I wondered if I was going to survive.

It was exhilarating and very noisy when I first jumped. I was so excited about realizing my dream that the free fall was over before I knew it. In the end, as I received high fives from the regular jumpers who were with me that day, I was in awe that I had made the decision to jump. Looking back, I hope everyone decides to make a big leap, in spite of their fear, at least once in their lifetime.

∞

Perceived fear can give us an adventurous thrill like with Janet's skydive, or it can be experienced in the quiet safety of our own homes. Imagine that you're sitting in the dark watching a suspenseful movie with nothing to protect you but your blanket. You're terrified. You screech at the slightest random noise in the house. Not even a toe slips beyond the edge of your blanket for fear that an unknown *something* will immediately bite it off. Yet even though you're absolutely terrified, you *love* the chill that runs up your spine.

So that begs the question of *why*. Why do so many of us love to feel the overwhelming rush of fear that comes with jumping out of planes, watching scary movies, and riding roller coasters? Why aren't we avoiding these perceived fears as much as we would *real* fear?

If we were to change up the above scenarios a bit, such as remove the parachute and imagine being pushed out of a plane, it might look and feel different. Would we, as we were falling to the ground, feel the same sense of freedom, the same thrill? Of course not.

Or if we were not *watching* a suspenseful movie, but actually *in* one of the situations depicted in the film, would we still enjoy that chill? Would the blanket *really* protect us from the unknown terror that's lurking around the corner? Of course not.

The answer to why we *seek* perceived fear and *run from* real fear is found in one word – safety. With perceived fear, *we know we're safe*. We're able to leap off of a cliff because we *know* a bungee cord will yank us back up before we hit the ground. We're able to take that roller coaster ride because we *know* the car is connected to a track and most likely won't derail. We can jump high on a trampoline because we *know* the net is there to catch us when we fall back down. So we grab on to the opportunity to experience the effects of fear, and yet still remain safe.

When we look at the world and all the fears, both real and perceived, contained therein, it becomes easier to see that while the *sensation* of fear can be thrilling and exciting, it can also be extremely terrifying and devastating, especially with all the unknowns we face in our daily lives.

Taking this all into account, perhaps we can define fear in a simpler fashion: *Fear is a lack of safety and a fullness of the unknown.*

When Real and Perceived Fear Collide

Anytime we reach out into the unknown, we're more than likely going to experience some kind of fear. We hesitate to move forward because there is no guarantee of safety. This is not only true in our physical world, but also, on a much deeper and more complex level, in our interior world – such as with our emotions, spirituality, beliefs and thoughts.

When we've been through something traumatic, we can be so impacted by fear at both a physical and emotional level that sometimes we become unable to differentiate between real and perceived fear. We hear a loud noise and are immediately thrown back, body and mind, into an intensely dangerous situation. We *feel* the danger, and we can't immediately tell if it is real or if we're actually safe in that moment.

This struggle with differentiating between real and perceived fear is shown in our next story with Samantha. We may not have spent two tours in Iraq like she did, but many of us have been through our own very real traumas and are left trying to figure out how to sort through our fears in the aftermath. Samantha gives us hope as she shares how she's learned to deal with her fear since returning home.

∞

BEFORE COUNSELING, I WOULD HEAR A SOUND AND MY FIRST THOUGHT WOULD BE THAT IT WAS A BOMB. I COULDN'T TALK MYSELF DOWN FROM IT. I WOULD PUT MYSELF IN A DARK ROOM SOMEWHERE QUIET AND AWAY FROM PEOPLE. MANY DAYS, I COULDN'T EVEN HANDLE BEING AROUND ANYONE.

- SAMANTHA

Samantha is a 32-year-old mother who was a military police specialist in the army and served two tours in Iraq. During deployment her main job was to guard Iraqi prisoners.

My biggest fear when working in the Iraqi prison centered on being a woman. I had fears around the way the Iraqi prisoners perceived women and even the way female soldiers are perceived in the U.S. I felt like women were probably enemy number one in the prison, especially because we were not only female, but also in positions of authority over the prisoners.

I was also afraid that the Iraqi prisoners had connections all over the world and my biggest fear was, and still is, that they would find out who I was and would somehow reach my family. It was an irrational fear, because we had to take off our nametags to get into the prison and only used our first names when interacting with each other. But I still worried – Would they know me? Would they discover my last name?

It was scary when the prisoners cursed at me and the other female guards and threatened us with physical violence if they ever got out. I remember one particular instance when a group of male prisoners arrived. Normally, the female guards processed the intake paperwork and didn't have to get physically close to the prisoners. But on this day, one of the male guards was out and it was just me and one other guy. We had about 20 prisoners come in all at once, and we were required to search them during intake.

As soon as I approached the first prisoner, he started to curse at me in Arabic. Our interpreter told me that I shouldn't touch the prisoner because he was saying that he had family all over the place. He continued to curse at me nonstop, and the interpreter was talking to me too, and my hands were shaking.

When we were done processing, I went into the break room and had a meltdown. I knew that I was just doing my job and didn't have a choice, but just thinking about it now still bothers me. Even though my fear might seem irrational, I still wonder where this prisoner is. What if he gets out? What if he's released and finds me? At the time, the prisoners' underground communication network was evolving and my fear was that they would figure out who I was and then somehow communicate with people back in the U.S. and that my family would be affected by it.

In my two tours in Iraq, I was never in the infantry or on the front lines, but I was in active combat. I've been shot at. I've seen a bullet rip through a little kid. I watched him die because he was just trying to get some food and happened to be in the wrong place at the wrong time. I still shut a lot of it out – I disengage from what I saw because I can't allow myself to go there. I'll look at my own children and try not to think about that little kid. The media desensitizes so much that some people really believe all Middle Eastern people are terrorists, but of course they're not. There are so many innocent people whose families are torn apart because of a war they aren't even directly involved with.

When I came home from Iraq, it took a couple of years to adjust. You see movies and hear stories of people coming back from war who think everything is a bomb, who freak out when they are driving down the road and a car in the next lane backfires. For people who haven't served, it's easy to think that it's not that bad, but it really is that bad. At first, I didn't want to drive and was terrified of loud noises. I would hear fireworks or backfires and my heart would start racing. I'd look around like somebody had been shot. It was raw fear.

Before counseling, I would hear a sound and my first thought would be that it was a bomb. I couldn't talk myself down from it. I would put myself in a dark room somewhere quiet and away from people. Many days, I couldn't even handle being around anyone. I would drive the 27 hours back home to my parents' house and spend the majority of my time there in my room by myself. People would come to see me, but I couldn't be around them. My breaking point was when my mom got upset because I couldn't be with the people who wanted to see me. I don't like to see my mom upset.

Counseling has been an important part of my healing and has taught me how to cope with my fear by teaching me how to step outside of my own head. I've learned how to determine if a fear is real or a manifestation of the past. Counseling has been a safe place to talk with someone who isn't involved with or related to me. I had to find that one person I could talk with and be one hundred percent real. I think a lot of people go to counseling and tell the counselor what they think the counselor wants to hear, which isn't going to help in the long run. They're not magicians. The reason why I had great success is because I went and wanted help. I wanted to change, so I opened up.

For me, living fearlessly is controlling your fears and your responses to them rather than letting those fears control you or your responses. I have learned that fear is an emotion based not on the present moment, but rather on our thoughts of what might be. So if I let those thoughts control me, then fear takes me outside of the present moment and into an imagined possible future. Living fearlessly isn't living in the absence of fearful thoughts - it is refusing to let those thoughts of negative possibility control my mood or actions in the present. And sometimes it means taking those fears and using them to push me into a proactive offense.

∞

Samantha's struggle after returning home from Iraq shows that we can't go straight to the effects of fear, such as wanting to hide in a bedroom, without also looking at their causes, such as having faced real danger. In order to help us break out of the boundary of our comfort zone, our fear boundary, it helps to be able to determine which fears are getting in the way of us moving forward. When we can do this, we are then able to name those fears and call them out for what they are in order to see which fears are real, and meant to protect us from doing something harmful, and which fears are deeply rooted inside of us, presenting no true danger and needing our active participation to help overcome them. Because while in the end there is no *guarantee* of safety, there *is* a strong probability of safety if we're not actually facing real danger.

In the next story, Mary Beth shows how real and perceived

fear are so interconnected. She shares how learning how to process perceived fear helped her sort through real fear when she found herself facing cancer. Her lesson shows us how when we practice overcoming fear in one area of our life, we can develop a strength and resilience that serves us well in other areas.

∞

I TRULY BELIEVE THAT PHYSICAL COURAGE IS SOMETHING THAT CAN BE TRAINED... IT'S THOSE LITTLE THINGS... THAT CAN PREPARE YOU FOR WHEN SOMETHING REAL HAPPENS IN YOUR LIFE AND YOU FACE REAL FEAR.

- MARY BETH

Mary Beth is a former combat engineer officer and Marine Corps veteran who was on active duty for eight years and served one tour in Iraq in 2003. She is now the director of a non-profit veteran organization that empowers veterans to keep serving and succeeding.

I truly believe physical courage is something that can be trained. I had a yoga teacher once call it "muscle over momentum." So when the momentum is carrying you in a certain direction, you can still use your brain to command your body to do something it doesn't want to do. Training my brain like this is something that I've proactively worked on.

Because I went to military school when I was 17, I had some opportunities at an early age to face perceived fears and be exposed to a physical courage that many young people don't encounter so early in life. When I was at the Naval Academy, we had to jump off a 10-meter tower into a pool. It wasn't such a big thing - people go bungee jumping and do crazy things all the time, but it was scary. Ten meters looks really high when you're standing on top of it at 17 years old. Some of my classmates could not command their bodies to jump, and they didn't graduate because of it. It might seem like a silly thing, but it does require physical courage. Very few people stand up there and think, "I'm dying to jump off of this thing!" It's scary.

It's these little things, like training your body to jump off a 10-meter tower, that can prepare you for facing real fear in life. Wherever I am, I'm constantly trying to mentally prepare myself in case something catastrophic happens. If there's a loud crack in the schoolroom or on the metro, I want to be ready. I know my body can only do so much, but I've always taken a proactive approach to scary situations and have trained my mind to beat perceived fear, knowing that even just doing the mental gymnastics can make us more prepared to deal with scary situations.

Throughout my time in the military I faced a lot of fears head on. I went to the Naval Academy for four years before entering the Marine Corps for eight. I chose combat engineering because I believed it was my best opportunity to be close to the front lines in case of conflict. All of those decisions scared the crap out of me. I knew what it would take to succeed at the Naval Academy, and I knew I might fail. But I was so driven and focused, I did it anyway. I knew with the Marine Corps I was taking a more difficult road than if I had chosen the Navy, but I did it anyway. When I chose to become a combat engineer, I knew what I was going to face both physically and mentally, but I did it anyway.

I entered the Marines with a lot of unknowns. It was a very competitive environment, particularly for women. I felt like I had to work twice as hard as the men around me in order to gain the same respect. That alone made me question whether I would succeed. I don't know if this is the part of my life story that addresses fear, though. The emotions at the time weren't so much based on fear as they were on adrenaline, and it was very fulfilling.

I was in Iraq, but my unit's mission didn't include going into direct combat with the enemy unless they came to us, which they didn't. I want to make sure I clarify that – there was no moment where I was raiding a building with my M-16 with people firing at me. That was not my combat story, and I'm in awe of the courage of those who took that on daily and still do.

There's a huge parallel between physical and mental strength. Maybe that's not true for everybody, but it certainly is for me. One thing I've always taken pride in, something that's given me mental strength and courage, has been making sure my body is prepared and strong.

I was diagnosed in January of 2013 with minor thyroid cancer, a cancer that is normally beatable and that 99 percent of people live through. But when you hear the word cancer, whether it's in your pinky finger or in your breast, it's a scary thing. Having my physical strength taken away from me during cancer treatment meant I had no control over my body, but I did still have control over my mind. I had to make a very conscious choice, similar to jumping off that 10-meter tower, to face my cancer with grace.

I'm not sure if real and perceived fear are different or if they're really related in the body – like I don't know if you can train yourself physically without also training yourself mentally. When you face a scary situation where you don't want to do something but do it anyway, that translates throughout your life. Resilient people tend to face personal challenges and overcome them with grace.

Getting my thyroid out involved two major back-to-back neck surgeries, which was pretty traumatic because it was a hard place on the body to have surgery. I was completely down for the count and my husband was on active duty at the time. So even though my mom stayed with me to help and was amazing, I had to do a lot on my own. I wasn't even allowed to walk enough to raise my heart rate, and I had three little kids.

After I recovered from surgery, I had to go five weeks where I wasn't producing any thyroid hormones. I couldn't have hormone replacement therapy, because the doctors needed to put my body into a hypothyroid state to prepare me for radiation. I don't mean to be dramatic, but during those five weeks I felt like I was dying. Like someone attached a tube to my arm and was draining the life out of me.

By the end of the five-week period, I couldn't climb a flight of stairs without taking a lot of breaks. I couldn't brush my teeth without taking a break. I had nothing controlling my metabolism or energy and I was depressed, because your thyroid hormones control that too. There were so many days when I wanted to lay down and just be done. I don't mean done like die. I simply didn't want to get up. It was too hard to get up and face having to parent and be present for three kids. It was hard to have a happy face for my husband so he wouldn't worry.

It was a scary time, because not only did I not know when I was going to feel better, but there was an element of fear surrounding me wondering if my cancer would come back if the treatment didn't work. I felt like I had completely lost control, like I was being dragged behind a truck. I could do nothing with my body physically. I wasn't even allowed to pick up my kids, so I had to find something that I could control that would help me to heal. I started with my nutrition. And as soon as I was physically cleared, I began working out with my at-home workout videos for 60 days. So, I found something in my life that gave me control, and I reached down and grabbed it.

If there's one thing I'd like to leave you with, it's this - we have to make a very conscious and physical choice to overcome things we're afraid of. We can't just let life happen to us. If we feel like we're getting dragged behind a truck, we need to find a way to grab onto the rope, pull ourselves up into the cab, and start driving.

∞

We learn from Mary Beth's story that when we shift our focus from being controlled by our fear to understanding our fear, we can use that knowledge to drive us forward and overcome things that might have previously seemed impossible. This is why it's so important to define fear and fearlessness and understand the very nature of fear. The more we know *what* fear is and how it shows up in our lives, the more we can understand how our own fears are connected to both our sense of safety and our ability to make decisions in life.

CHAPTER

2

KNOCK, KNOCK - WHO'S THERE: IDENTIFYING THREE FACETS OF FEAR

∞

The oldest and strongest emotion of mankind is fear, and the oldest and strongest kind of fear is fear of the unknown.

– H.P. Lovecraft

Fear is a lack of safety and a fullness of the unknown. While the *unknown* encompasses virtually every aspect of fear, in order to name our fears and claim them, we're going to break fear down further into three of its main facets - the unknown, known, and inevitable - and explore how they affect our responses to the way that we approach both real and perceived fears in our daily life.

These three facets of fear often overlap each other. For example, we might *know* the pain that comes from being hurt in the past, which causes us to fear the *unknown* that lies in the future. On the other hand, take a situation such as the upcoming birth of a second child. We *know* that we'll be facing the pain that comes with pregnancy and childbirth, and yet we *don't know* if everything will go as expected. Here, we have a fear of the *known* – pain – overlapping with a fear of the *unknown* – the health of our baby and the uncertainty of exactly how the labor and delivery will go. Will my baby be healthy? Will everyone be okay? And it's all compounded by the fear of the *inevitable* – the pain of the upcoming childbirth that we couldn't back out of even if we wanted to.

So in order to get unstuck from whatever it is that's paralyzing us from moving forward, we first need to dig deep in our own understanding of the ways in which what we fear is affected by the known, unknown and inevitable situations in our lives. Does our fear come from our past and what we've been through? Are we afraid because we just don't know what lies ahead? Are we scared of what's to come because we can't avoid it? By learning how these facets of fear impact our lives, we are able to better understand our own fears when it comes time to clearly name and claim them and then do the work to overcome them.

Fear of the Unknown

What makes an action movie so thrilling? What is it that has us holding on to our blankets or squishing in closer to someone on the couch during those intense moments? We *don't know* what's going to happen. We're biting our nails and clenching our fists as we wait to find out if the hero makes it, without ever having to worry about our actual safety, so our fear here is perceived. There's an unknown, but we know it's perceived fear, because it presents no real danger – either physical *or* emotional.

In real life, however, when we encounter the unknown, we often face fear that we'd rather avoid. We're hit with all the "what ifs," which can get pretty scary. This is especially true when those "what ifs" involve someone close to us and we have no control over our loved one's safety, which is what happened with Marie. She describes feeling as if her son was dead during the first two years of his incarceration, as all the *unknowns* surrounding his experience in jail gripped her with fear.

∞

IF YOU'RE GOING TO CONQUER YOUR FEAR, YOU NEED TO SAY "OKAY GOD, YOU'RE ALLOWING THIS. I SEE WHAT I NEED TO SEE. LET ME SEE IT WITH YOU." THAT'S WHEN I LET GO OF MY FEAR AND TURNED A CORNER.

- MARIE

Marie has been married for 32 years and has worked as a hairdresser for 36 years. She admits that she loves her kids "to a fault" and is passionate about helping them succeed and discover their own unique gifts.

As moms, we always have high hopes for our kiddos. We see their gifts, talents and faults, and we try to help them with these things as they grow. As they become pre-teens, we start losing some control over their lives, especially if they start doing things behind our backs or with their friends. I know this is what happened to me. And as a mom, I *knew* when something was wrong.

When my son Matt started making bad choices surrounding drugs and illegal activities, I could sense that I had lost control. I had homeschooled him to help with his ADHD and other problems that he struggled with his whole life, so to see this unfolding in a big muck of a mess was hard. He reached a point where he stopped taking my advice and leading a Godly life. Cops were coming to my door to take him in and calling me to come down to the station to pick him up after interrogations. This overwhelming fear overtook me. I could see the writing on the wall, and I knew where his choices were going to lead. I knew Matt was doing things that would probably land him in prison. And I knew enough about prison life that I didn't want my son in there.

So when Matt was arrested at 19 years old, I was afraid of not knowing what was going to come to pass. He was a sensitive soul deep down, so knowing his struggles with ADHD and knowing he wasn't a fighter - it all just made me so scared. I read somewhere recently that as moms there's a part of our DNA where we have an intimate physical connection with our kids. We know them inside and out, and we love them unconditionally. But when all of this was happening, it felt like that connection was somewhat lost. He wasn't listening or paying attention to me. He was lying to my face. He would look me in the eyes, and I would think he was telling the truth, but he would be lying. Looking back, I think it's because he was so into drugs that he actually believed his own lies.

The day the phone call came in that the cops had picked him up, Matt had already been missing for three weeks. I honestly didn't know if he was dead or alive. Then I found out that he was going to prison for six and a half years - *oh my heart*!

It's hard to describe what it felt like those first two years - it felt like he was dead to me, even though I knew he was alive. I knew there were many more years ahead, that the prison system had control, and that I was very limited in what I could do for him. I was afraid that he'd die without me by his side, that he was going to get beat up or treated badly by the guards. I felt so helpless. My God was all I had at this point, and the emptiness and fear inside just consumed me. I would sleep with my crucifix at night and beg God to protect my son. I didn't want him to be killed in there, but I also wanted him to change his heart and be the child of God that I knew he was created to be.

I remember the day I set foot in the prison to see him for the first time. I had never been in a prison before, and I was so scared because of the way they shook me down and made me feel like a prisoner myself. I was crying so hard and shaking. But I just had to trust despite how I felt. I'm very sensitive to spiritual surroundings, and I felt such darkness walking into that prison. Just knowing that this was where my son was staying made my stomach turn.

Fear of the unknown is so powerful. I've heard stories of inmates being raped and beaten to death. I've heard my son cry on the phone and tell me that he can't stay in there. And all I could tell him was, "Matt, the powerful thing you have is your prayers. You're in there, you can't control that, but you can keep praying." He's a real prayer warrior, but the fear of losing his grandpa or grandma or one of his parents while he's in prison is something he's talked about a lot. So many "what ifs."

My new fear is what will happen when Matt is released early this year. How is he going to be able to handle coming back into society? I know that it will be a struggle, that he will be marked and be on parole. I fear helping him adapt to the real world, but I've learned I have to take it one day at a time. I've learned that I'm not in charge, so I just give it to God because He is, and if we're going to conquer our fear, we need to say "Okay God, you're allowing this. I see what I need to see. Let me see it with you." That's where I turned a corner. It doesn't mean I'm not going to have sorrow or grief or fear. I just start trusting more quickly to walk with Him and into the fire.

∞

Marie's fear of the unknown was made real by her inability to know what was going on inside the prison and not knowing if her son was safe. There are so many things we can't control, especially when it comes to the fears surrounding what we don't know. As Marie shares, one powerful way to overcome these fears is to learn how to let go and trust at a deeper level. Trust in God. Trust in the process.

Let's look at another "what if." Imagine losing the love of your life while pregnant and having your whole world change in a single moment. This is what happened with Gisella, and her story provides a powerful example of how fear of the unknown can grip us in times of tragedy.

∞

> I THINK THAT FEARLESSNESS FOR ME WOULD BE NOT BEING AFRAID OF ANYTHING, STANDING UP OR MOVING FORWARD REGARDLESS OF HOW SCARED YOU MAY BE.
>
> - GISELLA

Gisella is a 37-year-old mom and an executive assistant at the

U.S. Department of the Interior. In May of 2014, she lost her husband Brad, an EMT captain, who had been suffering from cardiac issues for a while.

In May of 2014, I was commuting to work in Washington, D.C. and was pregnant with our third child, while Brad stayed home with our 18-month-old daughter. On the night before the day that forever changed my life, I remember coming home from work, kissing Brad goodnight, and going to bed.

The next morning, I was in the bathroom getting ready for work when my mother-in-law came to the house to help get our older daughter ready for school. She walked into the bedroom, where she found my husband unresponsive.

I remember hearing her shout, "Please wake up, please wake up!" Unfortunately, my toddler was also in the room as we were all hysterically trying to figure out what to do. We called 911, and the operator was trying to get us to do chest compressions. Luckily, my sister-in-law was there too and able to help. We were trying to do everything we could do to save him, but by the time the EMTs came they told us we had lost him.

It was all very shocking because I didn't expect to lose him that day. There was no indication that anything was wrong the day before, as I remember that he was acting normally. It wasn't like we knew something was going to happen; it was completely unexpected.

Our lives changed dramatically in that moment. I remember calling the pastor and him coming to the house and praying with us. My faith definitely helped get me through. I had just entered my second trimester when Brad died. And as scared as I was, I knew that this baby had to be healthy. I had to try to take care of myself, which was hard to do because I was so depressed. But I also knew I had to be strong for my other two children, so I pulled through.

The day I went into labor, my mother-in-law brought my husband's EMT uniform to the hospital. Brad had cut the umbilical cord for both our daughters, so having his uniform there made me feel like he was there in spirit. Everything went well with the labor and birth and when my son was born we laid him on Brad's uniform and took pictures. I think that moment helped all of us move forward in our faith. We knew that Brad was in a better place and we had this new baby to bring us joy.

As for now, I worry about my children a lot – I want them to be happy, not in pain. They're always going to miss their father, but I want them to feel fulfilled in life. I want them to know their father loved them, even though he's not here. I know Brad's death is always going to impact the kids, but we've been working to do everything we can to fill up this empty space.

So for me, fear is having anxiety about the unknown – not knowing what's going to happen and waiting for the other shoe to drop. And being fearless would be not being afraid of anything. It would be standing up or moving forward regardless of how scared you may be.

∞

Gisella's story is a beautiful lesson on how we can work through our fears in the face of the unknown and make the decision to keep moving forward, like she did after the death of her husband. Gisella stood in the face of her fear and made a decision to build a life for her children and family even after her husband was gone.

Although Gisella's fear was born in the wake of tragedy, we don't have to face a life-or-death situation in order to be faced with a deep paralyzing fear of the unknown. For example, we can face fear when we decide to quit a job we dislike or go out on a date with someone new.

Take the instance of a woman who has been through relationship hell. She's been hurt intensely, so the thought of even considering another relationship may emotionally paralyze her. Taking a chance on love means risking being hurt yet again. She just wants to know: Will it all turn out okay in the end? Will this story have a happy ending? Will he be her soul mate? This unknown fear fills the life of Kristina, whose first experience with love left her feeling unlovable and wondering if she could trust again. In her story we see the very real fears that can develop when past hurts are stacked on top of future unknowns.

∞

TO ME FEAR MEANS REJECTION, ESPECIALLY IN TERMS OF RELATIONSHIPS. IT FEELS LIKE DISAPPOINTMENT IN MYSELF, LIKE I'M NOT GOOD ENOUGH. I WOULD HOPE THE MESSAGE IN ALL OF THIS IS THAT WHILE EVERYONE HAS FEAR OF THINGS, WE CAN'T LET FEAR HOLD US BACK.

- KRISTINA

Kristina is 37 years old and single. Originally from the Miami area, she now lives in New York City and has a successful career as an emergency room nurse.

For the entire two and a half years that I was with my boyfriend Chris, I never felt good enough. He was the first person I was ever vulnerable with, and he often left me feeling rejected in so many ways.

From the beginning, Chris refused to put a label on our relationship - he'd tell me all the time that we weren't really dating, even though we were. Essentially what he was saying was that I didn't matter. He'd disappear for a week or so and then come back and disappear again.

I was so vulnerable when I met Chris. I just wasn't in a good place emotionally or financially, which compounded everything that happened. I had graduated from college and was living with my parents and was depressed and on medication. All that factored in to some of the decisions I made early on in our relationship. Looking back, I don't think I ever trusted him. He'd do things right in front of me, like text other girls whose numbers were saved as guys' names in his cell phone, and think that I didn't have a clue.

I moved in with Chris because I wanted to go to physical therapy school in Miami and wasn't in a financial place to move out on my own. I didn't know what to do, and I had never even been in a relationship before this one. It was hard because it wasn't what I had been expecting.

In high school, I felt like the only one who never dated, and it left me feeling unwanted and wondering what was wrong with me. I thought I would finally find that someone when I went to college, but even there I saw all my friends getting into relationships but it never worked out for me. Again, I felt unwanted, and it compounded my intense fear of rejection.

So by the time Chris came around, I had no foundation of romantic relationships from which to pull. And every time he cheated on me, every time he said things to me like "I'll never really love you. I'm never going to marry you. You're the reason I'm doing these things," I found myself believing what he said, blaming *myself* for the times he was unfaithful, and having this overwhelming fear of not even being lovable.

And yet in spite of all this history, I *still* felt terrible when we broke up. I didn't eat for weeks and didn't know what to do with myself. I would walk out of work at the end of the day feeling like a zombie. I had too much time to just think, so I'd go to the gym and workout for what seemed like forever. One time, I ran for so long that the treadmill actually turned off on me. I just turned it on again and kept running. I felt so empty.

Even though I was mad at Chris, a part of me wanted him back. I felt so alone and missed him, even though he had been so awful to me. I think all I wanted was an apology. I wanted him to admit that he had been wrong, because at the end he had blamed everything on me. He said it was my fault for finding out that he had cheated and that this was unforgivable. In retrospect I know this all looks so crazy, because obviously he's the "unforgivable" one. But at the time, it didn't *feel* that way. I blamed myself and couldn't help but wonder what I had done to make him not care about me anymore. What had changed?

Eventually, I forgave him because I knew that was what I needed to do for myself in order to move forward. One day I just made a decision that he wasn't allowed to control my emotions anymore. I was no longer going to allow him to make me feel so awful. It did take awhile to get there, but this was my turning point.

Dating after Chris has been wrapped up in so much fear. When I *do* find myself beginning to think that a guy is genuine, I quickly go to this default mode of not believing anything he says, of thinking he has an ulterior motive. It's all really messed up.

I know I come with some serious baggage, and I have to figure out how to cope with it or fix it. I've thought about this a lot, but don't know if I've come up with a good solution. I'm so cautious because I'm afraid I'll fall for someone again and that everything will be fine – until it's not. And then, I'm afraid that I'll allow myself to remain in something miserable once again.

I'm very comfortable in friendships with guys who are in relationships or guys who are married or even guys who I find unattractive, because there isn't any risk. I don't have to impress them or win their favor because I don't really care – I'm not looking at the potential for any sort of relationship. But if I meet someone with whom I think the end goal might be a successful relationship, well, then that scares me so much that I begin, once again, to self-sabotage.

To me fear means rejection, especially in terms of relationships. It feels like disappointment in myself, like I'm not good enough. I would hope the message in all of this is that while everyone has fear of things, we can't let fear hold us back. And we're not alone in our fears – all women have them and it's possible to overcome our fears and come out better for it.

So I hope the end goal is to encourage people to own whatever it is that is holding them back and just push through it. I still have all these fears about relationships, but that doesn't mean I've given up, even if I say sometimes that I have. I don't want to be single forever and I hope I find someone someday. I hope the reward outweighs the risk.

∞

Kristina's story shows how the complexity of fear affects us and how the unknown and the known can both play into our fears in a single situation. Her fear of what she went through in her last relationship – the known – affects her willingness to venture into a new relationship – the unknown – because she fears that her future is going to look like her past. We could have just as easily put her story in the next section on fear of the known, because like with so many of the stories throughout this book, Kristina's story reminds us that our fears – and our lives – are complicated.

Fear of the Known

Have you ever stepped on a sticker or a thorn? If so, then you understand the fear of the known, because you *know* that the sticker or thorn has to come out, and you *know* that there will be pain associated with it. You've experienced that quick chill that runs up your spine as you prepare to pull it out, knowing it's going to hurt.

We fear the *known* because we've already been through something, we *know* what it feels like, and we're afraid of going through it all again.

When we start to analyze the roots of our fear later in the book, it's important that we are able to pinpoint how the fear created by what we have experienced in the past can keep us from moving forward. Since our bodies and minds are hardwired to avoid pain and danger, we purposefully stay in a place where we feel comfortable. However, when we stay inside of our comfort zone, we're not only comfortable, but also unable to try new things or fully live out our dreams. As Mary shares in our next story, fear of the known can inhibit our ability to take risks, which is why sometimes we find ourselves feeling so stuck. The lesson we learn through Mary's story is how the consequences of what we've experienced in the past often leave us afraid of what might take place in the future.

∞

I HAD KNOWN THIS FEAR BEFORE, AND I KNEW WHAT TO EXPECT, AND INSTEAD OF GIVING ME SOME SORT OF COMFORT, WHAT I KNEW PARALYZED ME.

- MARY

Mary is 40-year-old teacher who is passionate about her work and lives for spending time outdoors and in the company of those she loves most.

I landed my first two teaching jobs rather easily, and so I honestly thought that as long as I worked hard and did the right thing, everything would always work out. So when I quit my dream teaching job to move across the country to live with my then-boyfriend, I just thought I'd get there and find a job. It was as simple as that. It didn't even occur to me that I might have cause to be afraid of finding work.

After the move, things didn't quite go according to plan. I applied for dozens of jobs over the course of months and when my savings started to run out, this completely unfamiliar fear crept into my life: "What would happen if I ran out of money? If I *never* found a job? If I had to admit failure, re-pack all my stuff and head back across the country, white flag waving in the air?" I was in uncharted territory and started to panic. Eventually I did end up landing a job. But this experience affected me in a way that would take a few years to really show up in my life.

Fast forward a few years and my now-husband and I decided we were going to make another cross-country move. Our move was contingent on me finding a good full-time job. So I started applying again. All over the place. And again, it didn't go well. In the rare case that I did land an interview, I was told, in some form or another, that I was either underqualified or overqualified for the position. I just couldn't find my place.

The fear really started to take hold. But now, it was a fear of something I had gone through before. And it was a lot scarier than the first time. Here I was again, facing the same situation and beginning to feel that what had happened after the first move was *not* a fluke, but my new normal. Maybe now, for the rest of my life, I was always going to have a hard time finding a full-time job that was a good fit for me.

I had known this fear before, and I knew what to expect, and instead of giving me some sort of comfort, what I knew paralyzed me. The story ends well. Kind of. I ended up finding a good full-time teaching position.

And yet now I *know* what it feels like to apply for so many positions and be told time and time again that I'm either underqualified or overqualified. I *know* the pain of rejection that comes with trying over and over again and coming up short.

This has all made me a little more cautious in the work that I do. I never used to think early on in my career about what would happen if I lost my job. I was so confident. I felt I was good at what I did and never acted in my daily work with any sort of fear.

I can't say that now. I let fear creep into my work almost every day. I don't speak up as often as I might otherwise. I say "yes" sometimes when what I really want to say is "no." I pass up opportunities to pursue work I most love in exchange for work that feels safe. I tell myself that it's just because I'm older now, because I have a mortgage to pay and people who depend on my financial stability. But if I'm really honest with myself, I know that it's because I have this fear as a result of what I've been through in the past and what I know could possibly happen again in the future.

There are days when this *known* makes me mourn my younger, more fearless self. And yet now, instead of this making me feel sad and helpless, it just means that I have to keep working all the time on not letting my fears be larger than my dreams. To me being fearless means recognizing that I'm afraid, but figuring out a way to still move through it and not let it stop me from living my life.

∞

Because of what Mary went through, her whole outlook on her professional life changed. She now makes certain decisions in her work for no other reason than that she fears that any boldness might leave her once again losing her job security and dealing with the aftermath of this loss. So her very strong fear of what she has known keeps her within her comfort zone.

Fear of the Inevitable

Cancer treatments. Imminent death. The terminal diagnosis of a loved one. Finding out we're unable to conceive a child. Childbirth. Graduation. Children growing up way too fast. There are so many situations in our lives where circumstances are thrust upon us, where we know we're going to go through something painful and that there's no way out of it.

Insert fear. One morning, we wake up and realize there is so much that's really out of our control. We can see the road ahead clearly and yet we feel like we're not the one driving the car. And the truth is that we're *not* in control. We *don't know* where the road will bend or how fast the car's going to travel. We only know that no matter what we may *want* to do, getting out of the car is not an option. We're moving forward, but we're also stuck.

So in order to understand our fear, we have to be able to ask ourselves, "Why am I afraid of this in the first place?" Many times, the answer is a complex recipe of all three facets of fear. For some of us, the scariest of the three facets is fear of the inevitable because when we're facing inevitable situations, we often lack control, which causes us to feel unsafe.

We see this complexity in Rachel's story, where fear of the inevitable gets mixed in with fear of the unknown and the known and creates a situation that's incredibly difficult to navigate through. The lesson here is that when we face inevitable situations that fill us with fear, we have no choice but to figure out a way to deal with what's coming ahead. We *do*, however, have a choice to either let our fear consume us or to walk with and through our fear.

∽

I THINK THE REASON WE FEAR THE INEVITABLE IS BECAUSE IT OFTEN TAKES SO MUCH EFFORT TO MOVE FORWARD AND FACE WHAT'S AHEAD. BUT WHEN WE REALIZE THAT THERE ARE ALL KINDS OF SUPPORT AVAILABLE TO US, AND WHEN WE SEE THAT WE HAVE SO MUCH STRENGTH WITHIN US, THEN WE CAN BE LESS AFRAID.

- RACHEL

Rachel is a 59-year-old physical therapist and mother of two children in their 20s.

When I think of fear, the first thing that comes to mind is not knowing the future because I like to feel in control. I recently found out that Phil, my 70-year old ex-husband and the father of my children, has throat cancer - a very deadly cancer. I immediately became scared for his life and also scared for my 25-year-old son, who has struggled with various addictions since he was a teenager. Phil and my son live together and really support each other not only financially, but also emotionally. So I fear that Phil won't have the support he needs as he faces the cancer because it's just so much in terms of the treatment and everything that comes with it. And I'm afraid that neither of them can handle it.

When I'm feeling afraid, the first thing I do is to try to find a solution. But with Phil's cancer, I can't fix it. I know that there's no avoiding what's coming and it's scary. I think the reason we fear the inevitable is because it often takes so much effort to move forward and face what's ahead. But when we realize that there are all kinds of support available to us, and when we see that we have so much strength within us, then we can be less afraid.

I think that when we're willing to move forward and face the inevitable in spite of our fears, the fear starts to dissipate. We can't let fear spin us back in the direction we've come from. We have to keep going in spite of the fear and figure it out. We have to keep moving forward, or sit still and be calm, but we can't let our fear overtake us.

∞

As Rachel's story shows, one of the reasons that fear of the inevitable is so scary is that we often have little to no control over what's coming. And for many of us, when we're faced with fear our initial response is to try to control whatever we can. The hope, though, is that the more we understand the nature of our fear, the easier it becomes to figure out how to deal with it.

The *inevitable* doesn't always have to be disastrous, however. It just means that we can't avoid what's coming next. Take a college student who is about to graduate. She's been in school for the past 16 years and her life is about to drastically change. Graduation – the inevitable – is right around the corner, a whole new "grown up" world is waiting for her, and all she can think is "what if?" "What if I don't find a job? What if I'm no good at the job I do find? What if I end up living back home with my parents, because I just can't make it on my own?"

On a more permanent and life-changing level, take a couple excited to grow their own little family. After trying and trying, then taking some tests, they come to discover that they're unable to conceive their own children. Suddenly they're living with a whole new world of fear that comes from the inevitable situation they're now facing, as we'll see with Annie. All Annie wanted was to have children of her own, but when she learned that she had unexplained infertility, she found herself facing fear as her dream of having a family of her own began to fall apart. Annie shows us is that even in some of our darkest moments, when we begin to look outside of ourselves, we can often find hope.

∞

THANKFULLY THE LIGHT BROKE THROUGH THE FEAR. SOMETIMES I SAW ONLY A GLIMMER OF LIGHT, BUT IT WAS THERE. HE WAS THERE, SHINING THE LIGHT FOR ME ON ONLY THE NEXT STEP AHEAD, BUT NEVER ANY FURTHER. ASKING ME TO TRUST.

- ANNIE

Annie is a 39-year-old mother of five adopted children who has been married to the love of her life for 16 years. She is passionate about her faith and loves to experience life through photography.

The first time I truly felt real fear was shortly after being married. I thought it was going to be the start of our family, but instead I was dealing with the humiliation of feeling like *everyone* was getting pregnant but me. After many doctor's visits and tests, we were told that we had unexplained infertility. It wasn't so much that we were told we had no hope. It was the anguish of exactly the opposite - having hope in each cycle that was dashed. Over and over again. Eventually, we just stopped charting altogether so I would be less conscious of where I was in my cycle - although a woman always knows.

I worried whether my marriage was going to be able to survive this stress. So that was my first big fear - our future as a couple, our future as we aged, and who was going to care for us. I feared what our Christmases were going to be like and how lonely we were going to be. The evolution of my thought process went something like, "Lord, please let it happen this month" to "Lord, help me not to want it anymore" to "Lord, help me to want Your will more than mine." I'm still working on that last one.

In those early years, I felt ugly and ashamed and wanted to just wallow and hide my sorrow from the world. I buried myself under a blanket – both literally and figuratively – to shut out the world of babies and pregnancy announcements. It was partly a matter of self-preservation, but also a result of not wanting to be a downer to every person I met. I wore my heart on my sleeve and couldn't attend church with families, let alone baby showers, without leaving in tears. I simply couldn't hide my sorrow. I was a buzzkill to everyone I talked to. Same sad story, different day.

I found myself pulling away from those who loved me and sinking deeper into the quagmire of bad thoughts. Taking the high road just seemed too hard. Unattainable. That was the stuff of saints, which clearly I was not. I fell deeper and deeper into darkness. I still bear deep wounds from that time and am very sorry for those I hurt along the way.

What doesn't kill us makes us stronger, and at some point I had to realize that. I was depressed, so I sought counseling and began taking medication. I was never suicidal, but there were times I was just like "Lord, deliver me from this life, because I just don't want to know a life without children. If you want to take me from cancer right now, sign me up." I thought that *cancer* would have been the best news – that's how deeply I had sunk. It was a complete white flag. *I don't care. Whatever.*

At some point I had to realize that God hadn't given me cancer, so if I had another 50 to 70 years on this planet, what did I want my legacy to be? What were they going to write about me in my obituary? Were they going to write about the fact that I was bitter and nasty, that when I didn't get my way I turned into a witch? Or was my legacy going to be that I was somebody who helped others walking the same journey, carrying the same heartache?

When I met other women who were struggling with infertility, I realized what a widespread problem it really is. So, I knew I had a choice. I could either be nasty about this and turn inward, or I could make a choice and ask myself how I was going to make lemonade out of lemons.

And I kept going back to what my obituary was going to read. When I would face a difficult moment, I'd ask that question: "What's my obituary going to say about me?" Every time I would sit down and look at the toilet to see I'd started another period, I was like "Blessed be the name of the Lord." Just like the book of Job, the Lord gives and the Lord takes away. We are called to praise His name in the good and the bad.

It took me years, and I do mean years, to come to that understanding. But once I did, I understood the definition of Christian joy. Christian joy isn't being happy in good times, it is being happy in bad times. Thankfully the light broke through the fear. Sometimes I saw only a glimmer of light, but it was there. He was there, shining the light for me on the next step ahead, but never any further. Asking me to trust.

So we made the decision to adopt. Starting the adoption processes itself was actually a relief from our infertility journey, because I was doing something that I felt certain was going to produce a baby in the end. When we started the process, all that fear morphed into something else because no matter how much money and time it might take, I felt we were moving in the right direction.

Even though the process wasn't scary overall, I certainly had moments of fear, especially with my first son Isaac's adoption because we almost lost his referral. The Guatemalan government shut down due to political unrest and put a stop to all adoptions, so we were waiting stateside for months to see if we were ever going to be able to adopt this kid whose picture was gracing our refrigerator. We had already gone to visit and had held him. We prayed a lot. I was 27 when we brought our first son Isaac home.

Our second son Sam's adoption came about two years after bringing Isaac home. We attempted another surgery and a few more infertility treatments in between. As much as our hearts were worn out from the lengthy first experience with Isaac's adoption, God was leading us back to Guatemala. Thankfully, Sam made it home exactly 10 months after we signed the application papers.

Our third child – and first daughter – Sarah came about as a result of lengthy prayer and a lot of angst. The boys were desperately praying for a baby. In my struggle, a wise priest counseled me, "If God wanted a different plan for you, He would change it in a nanosecond." I was scared, but again it was clear I needed to trust. I had to surrender that desire to God.

I came home that day, and prayed for nine days straight to find contentment in our family size. And then on the ninth day, an email popped up in my inbox informing me of a birth mother who was looking for a family. Would Mike and I be willing to step forward and offer a home to the baby? Sarah Faustina was born four months later.

This past year, we agreed to go to China to adopt. I wasn't exactly sure about this decision at first and my husband Mike and I dragged our feet for a long time. We finally decided that if we were going to do this, we just needed to pull the trigger at some point. At first it was like we were detached from the whole process of getting the paperwork ready. We didn't even share with people that we were adopting a daughter from China. We kind of kept everything quiet until we got the referral, and then the next day we saw another child's picture on our agency's website and felt drawn to adopt two children at the same time. There was this moment of elation as I realized, "Oh my gosh! We're having twins and it's so wonderful!"

I was floating for about a month, and then one night I was sitting there with Mike watching television when a scene of rural China came across the screen. And I had this moment of thinking, "What are we doing? Can I back out?" I don't know if it was so much fear that I was gripped with as it was this heart-palpitating anxiety.

Most of that spring and summer I just sat on my couch, staring at the crucifix and asking, "Please God, if this is not meant to be, please get me off this train before it's too late. I'm scared. I don't know how we're going to do this. I don't know how I'm going to have two special needs kids. I don't know how I'm going to bring home and learn how to parent toddlers." It was like all the world was dumped on my shoulders and I could not breathe. It was suffocating.

I'll never forget the overwhelming emotion that swept through our family the day we met our two babies. We flew to China with our other three children, walked into the area where the children were being held, and quickly scanned the room. But neither Marianna nor Joseph were among the babies there. So I whipped out my camera and started snapping away to capture the first moments of the families whose kids were present.

As a photography enthusiast, I was in my element and had gotten a little lost in my work when Mike pulled my arm and said, "She's here." I literally threw my camera at Isaac and walked over to a woman who was holding a little girl whose face I had been memorizing for the past five months. I told myself I would not break down. I would hold it together so as not to scare the babies. But the raw emotion just poured through me. I reached my arms out to her and Marianna leaned into me and dove into my arms.

Let me say that again - she *dove* into my arms! She seemed not the least bit distressed as she just stared at me and at the tear-streaked face of her new dad. The boys crowded around us, Samuel grinning from ear to ear and Isaac's eyes filling with tears as he buried his head in my shoulder, rubbing her back and saying, "Momma, she's here! She's perfect!"

What happened next is all a blur. The room was hot without any air-conditioning and there were babies crying and I was just a mess of joyful tears watching it all, experiencing it all. Then I saw a woman carrying a little boy with his back to me. By the hair I could tell it was our Joseph. I would have known that spiky hair anywhere. Then he turned his face in my direction and I grabbed Mike's arm for support.

He was clinging to the woman's neck, clearly overwhelmed by the noise and confusion of the moment. I was holding Marianna at the time so Mike put out his arms but Joseph immediately turned away. I knew he was scared and we weren't going to rush it. The orphanage worker handed Mike a lollipop to try to entice the child and handed Joseph over into Mike's arms. He just sobbed and arched his back and reached for the orphanage worker. My heart clenches even now as I think about that moment. He was so scared and confused and it just broke my heart. But we knew we had to persist.

Joseph's caregiver, clearly accustomed to the scene, made Joseph a bottle and placed him in my arms. I then settled down on a chair to feed him. He hungrily drank from the bottle while his eyes locked on mine. He was tolerating me for the moment but his little body was tense. The bottle helped to calm him down and before long he put his little head down on my shoulder and promptly fell asleep.

It was an existential moment. I looked around the room at the other families – some still struggling with crying babies, others able to arouse a giggle from their new little ones, and all of us overwhelmed by the whole event. How many different paths had led us all to this room on this day and with these children. But it had all been planned from the moment of Creation. Tough as I knew this day and the next few days were going to be, each one of the parents in that room was born for this. For them.

To be honest, I hate it when people tell me, "Oh, you guys are so awesome for what you do." Honestly, our kids are what saved us from being those bitter people that our obituaries were going to be written about. Our kids saved us from that. And there was such tremendous grace there. Adoption is not for everyone, but I believe that if we're called to something, God gives us the grace. I never thought I would ever be able to be the mom of a special needs child and now I have two. There's *no way* I would have done this on my own. The only way I was able to do this was through grace and responding to grace.

Now, I've found myself constantly thanking God for this trial. I have a whole new perspective. I used to sit behind parents and families at church in the early days of our marriage. I would just look at those big families and think, "They are so lucky, they have no problems in the world, they have everything that I have always wanted." But I never saw the struggle, I never saw the crosses they bore. And now with our family of five, I think, "Oh to be able to have a conversation uninterrupted with my husband just once."

Our cups overflow.

∞

Annie's story gives us a lesson on how we can deal with the different facets of fear – the unknown, known and inevitable – when they show up in our lives. We can become consumed by our fear, or we can clearly name the fears that show up, recognize the place they have in our lives and choose to create a different ending.

Sometimes in order to clearly name our fears we need to step back from our immediate circumstances, like Annie did when she imagined how her obituary would read. Doing so gave her a clear wake-up call and encouraged her to do something different.

In order for us to be able to move forward, we need to know what's keeping us stuck. When we not only understand what fear is, but personally make sense of why we fear and how the facets of fear pertain to our own stories, we can then unravel some of the complexity of fear as we claim it and work to understand its deep roots.

CHAPTER

3

GOING ON A FEAR HUNT: DISCOVERING THE DEEP HIDDEN ROOTS OF OUR FEARS

You're imperfect and you're wired for struggle, but you are worthy of love and belonging.

– Brené Brown

Do you ever take a look at some of your deepest fears and conclude that they're completely unfounded? It's easy to look inside and think that somehow we're weaker, less capable, or even less worthy because we're gripped by fears that we often feel are invalid in the first place.

Well, my friend, I've got some *great* news for you. There is actually *good* reason for our fear, and we are not alone. There is a reason *why* we're often afraid to take that next step, or to even think about taking it. There's a reason why we feel terrified to let down certain walls we've built over time. Why we're not able to venture out into the unknown and cross that fear boundary.

In order to understand the reason behind our fear, let's dive into a bit of science so we can help bring to light why we're afraid to move forward, what's been holding us back, and how we can come to understand and claim the deep hidden roots of our fear. As we dig deeper we will find that many of these fears are actually tied to our basic human needs.

How Our Needs Affect Our Fears

Abraham Maslow, a well-known psychiatrist from the mid-1900s, studied what humans need to not just exist, but thrive. From his research, he created the Hierarchy of Needs Theory, which shows that all of our needs are not created equal. There is a specific hierarchy as to how our needs must be met, starting with the most basic needs and moving on to the more complex ones. In short, to truly live a fearless and free life, our needs have to be met in a particular and predictable order.

Starting at the lowest level of this hierarchy, the physiological level, we find the needs tied to our physical survival - air, food, water, sleep, excretion, etc. If we take any of these away, such as oxygen or food, we will most definitely die.

On the second level, the safety level, we're still looking at some basic needs for survival - like having clothes for our backs, a job to be able to provide food, a place to live, our health, and security of body, among other needs - but we're no longer talking literal life and death. Without these needs being met, it's unlikely that we will die, but we most likely will not thrive.

The third level of Maslow's hierarchy is where we find the roots of a lot of the fears we're diving into in this book. The importance of the needs on this level might surprise you at first, because there is a common misconception that the needs listed here aren't true *needs*. And because of this misconception, it naturally follows that some people might believe our fears associated with the third level are misguided, unimportant, frivolous, or even wrong. You see, this is the level where we find our basic human need for love and belonging.

Yes, we were *created* to have a desire for love. We were built to have that longing to be part of something bigger. We were designed to long for those intimate friendships and unguarded relationships. Isn't that *great* news?

When we take a good look at the whole picture, we can see that as long as all of our needs are provided for – as long as we can eat, breathe, sleep, have a place to live, a job, a house, security of body, etc. and as long as we feel like we belong and are loved – we *feel* safe.

Connecting Love and Belonging to Safety and Fear

Remember how we defined fear again? *Fear is the absence of safety and a fullness of the unknown.* So if we want to understand *why* we fear and how we can work through these fears, we have to acknowledge that lack of safety is – by definition – fear's foundation.

If any one of our basic needs is threatened, we suddenly feel unsafe. Where we should have a sense of security, we now have the cold, dark, chilling *lack of safety* – a.k.a. *fear*. And at this third level of Maslow's hierarchy, our need for love and belonging is so strong that when this is stripped away we're often left grasping for some sense of knowing that we are lovable or feeling that we belong at all. And although we might not be experiencing any form of physical harm, we still don't *feel* safe.

The fear we feel when our need for love and belonging isn't met sometimes causes us to go places we swore we'd never go in the first place, as we'll see in our next story from Gabriella. Her story shows the connection between Maslow's third level, the fears we battle, and the importance of both recognizing this connection and working through the fears that emerge when we don't feel emotionally safe.

∞

I DO THINK IT WAS MY FEAR OF NOT BELONGING, OF NOT BEING LOVABLE THAT OPENED THE DOOR THAT DAY WHEN MY "FRIEND" FIRST MESSAGED ME. I THOUGHT I WAS STRONG AND THAT I WOULD NEVER GO THERE, BUT BECAUSE OF MY BROKENNESS, I DID, AND NOW I'M PICKING UP THE PIECES.

- GABRIELLA

Gabriella has been married for nine years. She is a mother of three boys and works part-time as an interior designer.

Fear for me is darkness. Loneliness. The darkest period of my life began about four years ago when my family went through major financial hardship. My husband lost his job, so we packed up our three children and moved in with my retired parents. New town. New job. No space. I found myself without any friends. My only sibling lived across the country, and I felt very alone.

No matter what I did for my parents, it never felt good enough. I could never stay on top of the house. I struggled with getting dinner on the table with my infant being so demanding, and the children would often be noisy, which rattled my parents' patience. My husband was looking hard for a job, so we were depending on my parents for income, and each day got harder and harder when no job opportunities opened up.

It was a period in my life when I felt completely worthless and unlovable. All I wanted was to be able to move freely in my own space, but I felt trapped. I had to hide more and more of who I was in order to conform to who I thought everyone *wanted* me to be. As I felt myself slipping away, I began to struggle with suicidal thoughts: "It would be better if I was dead. I could make it quick and be done with everything. I could be free." It was such a dark time in my life and I was so lonely and afraid.

Around this time, I joined Facebook. I had heard my friends talk about it and it sounded interesting, so I signed up. Within a couple of months, I got a message from a friend. "Hey, Gabby, how are you?" It was one of my sorority brothers from college. I was excited to get into a conversation with someone, because

I was really struggling with the reality of my daily life and just wanted an escape, and so we started to chat.

At first, it was very innocent. Just knowing someone *wanted* to talk to me was like adding a small ray of sunshine to the darkness, and slowly I began to seek out the sun. It wasn't long before he started pushing boundary lines. I would insist that I wasn't interested in going there. I just wanted the friendship. But whenever we talked, I felt cared for, and my need to know that I was *wanted* led me to crave the attention.

He would disappear when he saw that I wouldn't bend on the boundaries, and because I was already feeling so lonely, this left me feeling even more depressed. Looking back, it seemed like he was "punishing me" for not falling into his trap. And it *was* a trap, but I was naively blind to it.

He would reappear, and we'd start chatting, and again, I would feel like I was wanted. And then he'd start to pressure me. My feelings of being unlovable and unwanted were growing daily, as I struggled to make new friends and stay connected with my husband as he was going through his own stuff. It felt like my husband was checking out and wasn't able to give our family what we needed. I just felt like nothing in my life was working. So this old college "friend" kept pushing the boundary lines, and I wore down bit by bit, until one day I finally gave in.

One thing led to another, and before I knew it I was having a very twisted online affair. I would try to step back and stop it. I'd block him. I'd try to convince my husband that we needed to move out and find our own place, but financially it just wasn't possible. I'd fall into deep depression again and unblock my old "friend." He'd message me.

It was a horrible cycle, and my life began to spin out of control. I didn't *want* this. I *knew* it was wrong, but I was so terrified of the nothingness. I was afraid of being completely unlovable. I felt so worthless. Family of five, living with my parents. No job. Welfare. Constantly being reminded that I wasn't enough. I was living my own personal nightmare every minute of every day. So I snapped. I became someone I didn't recognize and started living this other life.

I did a lot of things during that time that I really regret. My husband and I are still working through the pain and the heartache, but my hope is that we will both eventually heal.

I hope in sharing my story that women reading this will see that when we are afraid of not being loved and of being unwanted, we often travel down roads we never imagined that we'd travel. So I do think it was my fear of not belonging, of not being lovable that opened the door that day when my "friend" first messaged me. I thought I was strong and that I would never go there, but because of my brokenness, I did, and now I'm picking up the pieces.

To me, being fearless is *knowing* that I'm loved and that I belong, even during times when it's so hard to feel this way. It's being secure enough in who I am to not care what other people think. I don't know if I'll ever be fearless, but I am hopeful that whatever I go through in my life going forward, I will find a way to heal and to come out stronger on the other side.

∞

Gabriella's story is a lesson in how many of our deep-rooted fears are directly related to whether we feel loved and lovable, feel as though we belong and are accepted, and feel connected to something bigger than our own isolated experiences. *These* are the fears that stop us from following our dreams or achieving our biggest goals, and sometimes from answering those quiet – but important – longings of our hearts. These are also the fears that can drive us to build walls so high that it seems nearly impossible to tear them down.

Our fears as they're connected to love and belonging don't always make sense to us. It's incredible how we can feel like we don't belong or are not accepted, even when we know for a fact that we are. In our next story, Jatana shares some of the fears she felt as a new mom. Whether you're reading this as a mother or not, one of the important lessons we can learn from Jatana's story is that even when it looks on the outside like someone has everything she's always wanted, often she's still battling deep and real fears. Her story reminds us that we should never minimize someone's fears just because it might look on the outside like she's living the life she's always dreamed.

∞

IT'S MY FAITH THAT REMINDS ME THAT EVEN THOUGH I HAVE THESE PASSIONS AND DREAMS, AGAIN — THEY'RE NOT ON MY TIMELINE, THEY'RE ON HIS. HE KNOWS MY HEART. HE KNOWS MY DESIRES.

- JATANA

Jatana is a 35-year-old mom of two boys who has been married to the love of her life for 11 years. She grew up in a broken home and always dreamed of living the American Dream. She was crowned Mrs. Virginia in 2015.

I'm most afraid of not being enough in all aspects of life. I'm also afraid of disappointing people – my kids, my husband, my friends, my family, my team I work with. In my business, I'm afraid of setting high expectations and not meeting them.

One of the darkest times in my life was right after having kids when I felt like I completely lost my identity. I think a lot of moms get to this place when they have their first child – they're not sleeping, they're not showering, and they're unable to detach themselves from their baby. I remember thinking, "I'm a new mom and I have kids and I have a home and I have a loving husband and this sucks." I was miserable and couldn't understand why. It's so confusing, but I was in a really dark place.

One of my biggest struggles has been expecting to feel a certain way and then just not. I was so disappointed in myself and even thought that maybe I wasn't created to be the mother of my child if I wasn't enjoying motherhood. I didn't know how to find the joy I knew I should be feeling. I think a lot of women go through postpartum depression and wonder, "What's wrong with me? Why can't I force myself to be happy with this?" It is a really scary place to be.

I remember nursing my son Joshua and just crying, "God this is what I've always wanted. I went to school and I have this kind husband and a home and stability. And now I have this child, and I'm not happy. What's going on?"

In that moment, I got this overwhelming feeling that I needed to be content right in the place where God had me. And I remind myself of this when I get in a funk about where I am or why I'm not where I think I should be in life. God reminds me, "Jatana, I have a timeline for you. And my timeline is more important than your timeline. So you need to be patient and trust that I know what is best for you."

So I try to be patient when I begin to think that I've wasted my time because I haven't met certain goals I've set for myself. And it's in these moments that God reminds me of the same thing over and over again, just like when I was sitting there, nursing my baby – it's not on my timeline, it's on His. It's about the people I'm interacting with and it's about my growth. He knows my heart. He knows my desires. It's my faith that reminds me that even though I have these passions and dreams, again – *they're not my timeline, they're His.*

∞

Jatana felt lost in a world where she thought that she was *supposed* to be happy, but didn't *feel* happy, which fed into her biggest fear of not feeling like she was enough. It was only when she decided to let go and trust that she found peace.

Why Just "Getting Over It" Doesn't Work

Exposing our emotions can make us vulnerable. When we open up on any level about our need to feel loved or to belong, we run the risk of being told to simply "get over it," as if this deep-seated need for love and belonging shouldn't play an important role – if any role at all – in who we are and how we're showing up in the world. And so we often believe these lies, telling ourselves that, well, maybe we really *should* just "get over it," that maybe we're not *normal* to feel the way we do. That we just need to shake it off and keep moving forward – to soldier on.

The problem with shaking it off and soldiering on is that we tend to stuff our fears into a box we've so carefully hidden within the depths of our hearts and our minds – a box where we stash our deepest secrets, hurts, and painful memories that we'd rather forget. When we're hurt, we tend to open up the box as fast as we can, stuff the fear inside, lock it up tight, hide the key, and carry on, often denying the fact that deep down, we're *still* hurt, that our feelings *are* valid, that these hurts *still* affect us, and that, *yes*, it's okay to process them and to try to answer the question – what's next?

In Karen's story, we see how fear started showing up when she was just a young girl and still affects much of her life. Her story is a lesson in how often the fears that show up in our everyday lives are deeply rooted in our past.

∞

IT'S BEEN SO LONG SINCE I FELT TRULY FEARLESS, WHICH IS WHY IT MAKES ME FEEL A LITTLE EMOTIONAL TO EVEN THINK ABOUT IT. I THINK FEELING FEARLESS WOULD HAVE TO BE FEELING BLESSED AND HAPPY, KNOWING THAT I AM ENOUGH. IT'S BEEN A LONG TIME SINCE I'VE FELT THAT WAY.

- KAREN

Karen is a mother of two daughters, a lover of Crossfit, and a former middle school math teacher who retired from teaching to pursue a dream of wellness coaching. She now is a successful business owner and leader of a team of mostly women, whom she helps to achieve goals related to fitness and freedom.

What's interesting to me is that there are so many different facets of fear – like there's fear that takes my breath away, fear that raises my heart rate, and fear that makes me cry. When I hear the word fear, the first thing that comes to mind is just sadness, honestly. Isn't that weird? I associate fear with something that is extremely paralyzing or limiting. And this saddens me.

Because of how I was raised, I started processing fear when I was really young. I grew up in an alcoholic home where I often faced real fear. I remember being three years old and fearing for my life while out on a boat with my father who was drunk out of his mind. When we got back to shore, my mother kept crying while holding my then 18-month-old sister. So that was fear, but also sadness.

Knowing my own struggle with fear and how I started processing it at such a young age, I worry for my little girls. We almost lost my brother two years ago and my daughters had a couple of years where every time they saw their uncle, he was in the hospital. I wondered with their limited life experiences how they processed it all. Fast forward to this year – I've had more of the same fears for my daughters, as I recently miscarried twice. I worried about what they thought when I kept saying "Mommy doesn't feel good. She has to go back to the doctor to get better."

I've been so afraid of failing myself, of not being able to get out of the sad place that I was in after losing my babies. I was so frustrated that I couldn't just snap out of it. But my heart was so full of hurt and suffering, and the hormone changes were chemically affecting me as well. I was unsure of whether I was going to get through it all. And now I have the fear of trying again. What does trying again look like? Am I ever going to be ready to do that? That's where I know I have to let my dream be bigger than my fear.

When I was a teacher I was extremely fearful of not doing right by my students. I was fearful that they wouldn't be prepared for the things I thought they needed to be prepared for. I feared a lot for them for personal reasons too, because they didn't have all rainbows and butterflies at home. I grew up as a silent sufferer in an alcoholic home and always had a smile on my face, so I knew in my class I probably had some of those same students and it hurt so much to know I couldn't reach them all.

In my wellness coaching business, I've had to work hard to overcome my biggest fear of not serving others in the way they need to be served. I'm afraid I won't meet expectations and sometimes I get stuck in that fear. It's a fear of my own failure, but it's also a fear of failing others. I also have some limiting fears surrounding success in my business. Like what if I do everything I know I need to do to be successful and I still don't hit a goal? This is when it's easy to self-sabotage so if I don't reach my goal I have something to blame it on.

I also have a fear of having my family in the public spotlight. I'm very public now when it comes to social media. We live in a nice home in a nice area, and we have two girls. There are some sick people in the world, and that crosses my mind too – Should we have a gun? Should we upgrade our security system? Do we need to do more to keep them safe? These are fears that wouldn't even cross my mind if I didn't have such a public presence online.

It's been so long since I truly felt fearless, which is why it makes me feel a little emotional to even think about it. I think feeling fearless would have to be feeling blessed and happy, knowing that I am enough. It's been a long time since I've felt that way.

At the end of the day, I do believe fear is a choice. We create and give in to fear when we focus on obstacles, negatives, and things out of our control. Taking actions, focusing on the positive, and having faith can help us move through our fear and get to the other side of it. Acting in spite of our fear is a choice.

∞

Understanding these deep hidden roots of our fear, like we see in Karen's story, is a very important part of the process of working through the fears we have now, because it's hard to move forward if we're unable to pinpoint those areas in which we need to change and grow.

Naming Some Root Fears

Let's be bold here and just name some of those fears that are so intricately connected to our inherent need for love and belonging. We know *what* fear is and *why* our fears affect us so deeply, so by giving more specific names to these fears, we can get one step closer to experiencing the freedom we feel when we finally overcome them.

Some of these common fears that tend to hold us back are fear of rejection, fear of being unlovable, fear of not belonging, fear of failure, fear of humiliation, fear of being unworthy, fear of being forgotten or unnoticed, and fear of being judged. You name it. The list goes on.

We may not see or feel it, but fear can paralyze parts of our personality and our drive that we had no clue were even affected by its grip. So even though it may not seem like going after that job promotion is directly tied to our deep-rooted fear of rejection, it could be that's *exactly* what's stopping us from moving forward.

This fear of rejection is illustrated in our next story, where we get a good look at how this fear can affect us in a way we often can't see until we're looking back. Elizabeth shares how she found herself wanting to be accepted by an Iraqi prisoner who had committed some heinous crimes. Even though most of us haven't been through an experience quite like Elizabeth's, her story shows just how deep our need for acceptance and belonging goes and illustrates the fear that often accompanies this need. It might be easy to think that if we were in Elizabeth's shoes we would never have felt the way she did, but if we listen closely we might be able to see why she ended up seeking acceptance in the most unlikely of places.

∞

I GOT TO A POINT WHERE I REALLY WANTED THIS PRISONER TO TRUST ME, TO ACCEPT ME. IT WAS HARD TO RECOGNIZE THAT I WAS BEGINNING TO THINK THAT I WANTED TO BE FRIENDS WITH A MASS MURDERER.

- ELIZABETH

Elizabeth is 31 years old and has recently chosen an artistic path in life and is loving it. She worked for six months in a hospital in a detainee facility in Iraq, a holding area for prisoners. She was responsible for coordinating patient care among doctors, medics, and detainees.

I was in a place where I got first-hand experience with Iraqi people. I worked directly with the interpreters, as well as the Iraqi detainees. Some of the detainees were very bad men, and some of them were just in a bad spot when they were detained. The relationship that was built between the medics and prisoners – these Iraqi people who were supposed to be our enemy – was strange. It felt like we were treating our neighbors, people who lived down the street, and giving care as if they were our own. It was hard sometimes to have that separation, knowing that one of the prisoners could do something malicious or hurtful to us when all we were doing was trying to help them.

It's hard to name the fear surrounding all of this because there were so many things that played into what was going on. The army trains you that no matter who they are, if they are a threat to you, they're your enemy. So that means if a little kid is standing by the side of the road with an AK-47, then that kid becomes my enemy. This training is meant to save lives, but it's also kind of scary. So to think about what you're taught, and then to think about how you're raised to treat others the way you want to be treated – to be nice, to be helpful, to not treat others with disrespect – it leads to a battle of yourself versus what you've been trained to do. I can't even really give this fear a name.

The fear of not being liked or loved, the fear of rejection, doesn't necessarily just have to do with wondering if someone else likes you. On a personal level I wasn't at war with these prisoners, but our countries were at war. Even though I was in a war zone, my job was to help people. But at the same time, I knew that I couldn't become too complacent because there was real danger surrounding what the prisoners might do. I was there to help them, but I had to be on my guard. I struggled with this constant back and forth between wanting to help them and not wanting to see them as the enemy, but then also having that fear in the back of my mind of what they might do.

I fought a continual battle between doing what I had been trained to do and longing for social connection. I also fought the guilt that came with providing medical care to prisoners. Sometimes it's hard to justify treating someone who has done heinous things in his life, who you know has killed a lot of people. And yet even when I knew what a prisoner had done, I still got to this place where I wanted to be accepted by him.

At one point, there was a particularly notorious prisoner in my care and when I found out who he was, I wondered why we were even holding him. One of our sergeants assigned me the job of delivering this prisoner his medication and food daily. The first day I was so terrified I was in shock. I walked into his cell, accompanied by two guards, and saw him chained to the wall. He looked like any of the other men we were holding, and so it was hard for me to really wrap my head around the extent of the crimes and murders I knew this man had committed.

As the days went on, I had to do my job in spite of my fear. I still had to give this prisoner food and medicine and make sure that he was abiding by the rules. He was in solitary because of his notoriety, and when you're dealing with anyone in solitary you can't help but think about what life would be like in that cell, no matter who the person is. You start to forget what they've done, or at least put it on the back burner.

In my eyes, he started to be just a person who needed medical care, a man who was in need of something that I provided for him every day. That was my job as a medic. So you start to think about it, how lonely it would be to be in that cell. No matter what his crimes were, I got to a point where I really wanted this prisoner to trust *me*, to accept *me*. It was hard to recognize that I was beginning to think that I wanted to be friends with a mass murderer. "Friends" is probably the wrong word, because in a patient/medical provider relationship you have to remain at a very professional level. You have to be aware and conscious of not letting down your guard for even one minute.

I think at one point I felt like there was something wrong with me for feeling like I needed his acceptance. I wanted to not care about what he thought of me. I wanted to be able to just do my job and move on, but I'm not the kind of person who goes around not liking someone. So my biggest lesson here was that everyone craves acceptance from others, no matter who they are. Even when we know that a person has done bad things, he or she is still a person.

For me, being fearless, especially in these situations, is a combination of being both knowledgeable and brave. It's about understanding why I'm afraid and then getting the bravery either to step full force toward it or deal with that fear. Making that move to be brave enough to handle whatever it is that I'm facing is fearlessness to me.

∞

The lesson we learn from Elizabeth's story is that our need to be accepted and to belong is so strong that it's practically coded into our DNA. Have you ever found yourself wanting or needing acceptance from someone and wondering "Why do I care so much? Why am I even allowing this person to occupy space in my brain, not to mention wanting their acceptance?"

It's uncanny how so much of what we do in life is connected to this very concept, causing us to question: "Am I loved by this person or group? Do I really belong here?" When we remove ourselves from a situation and take a look at our actions from the outside, we can see more clearly how fear affects us when we're not accepted and feel we don't belong. And when we can actually *see* how it affects us, we begin to understand what we need to change in order to let go of the fear that is keeping us stuck.

Our innate need for love and belonging becomes even more clear in this next story where Anne shares her own deep desire for belonging after finding out that she was adopted. It was only when she was able to come to terms with how her adoption had impacted so much of her life and her need to belong that she was able to really start healing and finding peace.

∞

IT'S HARD TO FIND A WORD TO DESCRIBE THAT EMPTINESS. I KNOW THAT RIGHT THERE STAYED WITH ME FOR SO LONG, AND I FELT UNLOVABLE AND NOT GOOD ENOUGH AND JUST THIS CRAZY DESIRE TO BE ACCEPTED.

- ANNE

Anne is a 41-year-old mom of girls and a military spouse who is passionate about natural childbirth and overcoming obstacles.

I was born, I think, on January 21, 1975. That's the date on my handwritten birth certificate. My birth mother gave me up for adoption at birth, and I have no idea what happened to me from January 21 until March 15 when my parents adopted me.

From my earliest memory of knowing I was adopted, I remember feeling a sense of really wanting to be *from* my family. I don't have a recollection of a sit-down talk where my parents told me that I was adopted. At the same time, I don't remember ever *not* knowing I was adopted, so I know my mom told me when I was very young. I remember lying in bed crying when I was a small child, wanting so badly to be *from* my parents.

I didn't really understand why it hurt so much, except that I knew I wasn't *from* them. And the fact that it was something I could never change just hurt so badly and is something I've held on to for a long time. I never felt the strong family bond growing up that I craved. I never looked into the eyes of another blood relative until my daughter was born, which floored me. It was so strange when I looked into her eyes. I didn't know how it was going to be until it happened.

Recently, I've really had come to terms with how being adopted has affected my life. I've always just pushed it off like it's not a big deal, but I honestly think I've made a lot of decisions because of a desire to belong. I've had abandonment issues and have made many choices in my life because of my fear of being rejected. I've always had this fear that I'm not going to be loved, but I never really dug deeper into what this fear actually meant until more recently.

Growing up, I had such a distorted view of relationships and love and had this deep need to be loved by whomever. I definitely had an issue with promiscuity and getting into bad relationships with men who were terrible for me, men I had no right being with. It took me a long time to forgive myself for that. From the time I was in high school through my mid-thirties I also had a significant drinking problem. And in high school, I was very violent. I broke bottles over people's heads. I smashed a mug into an ex-boyfriend's face to the point where he needed stitches. My parents were like, "Okay, you need to go to counseling. We don't know how to deal with you anymore. You're out of control."

I remember when I sat down with this counselor and the very first thing she said was, "You're adopted, aren't you? I think that has a lot to do with the things that you're doing." As soon as she said this I completely shut down. I was like, "How dare she not get to know what's going on with me?" I was 17 years old and angry and didn't want anyone to put a label on me. I was like "No, that has nothing to do with it. I'm just making bad decisions because I'm 17."

After that first counseling session, I was so angry and just wanted to hide my adoption. I didn't want people to say that I made bad choices *because* I was adopted. I didn't have any control over being adopted and I wanted to *own* all my bad choices. But now that I'm older and wiser, I can look back and see that it really goes so much deeper than what I wanted to admit at the age of 17.

In some ways, I started my life feeling like an underdog because I thought my birth mom didn't want me. I have no way of *knowing* for sure what my birth mother was feeling when she was carrying me, but I do believe that she probably wasn't happy and positive the entire pregnancy. I think she knew she was going to give me up, and I know the energy and feelings of angst that were in her were also in me when I was born. It's like when you're pregnant and you work hard to maintain a positive attitude because you know your baby can feel your energy. So I'm sure she was filled with angst, but I'm also sure she was still filled with love. My birth mom was pregnant in 1975, so I know she could have had an abortion, but she didn't. And so I'm just grateful to be alive.

I have this gratitude in my heart now for my birth mom that I never knew until I had my own daughters. I never realized what it was like to carry a baby until it happened to me. I just know that it must have taken a lot of selflessness and love to carry me for nine months, even if maybe she had wished she wasn't pregnant. And I think she must have lived with this tension for her whole pregnancy and maybe for my whole life.

The big healing in my own life, when I began to let go of my own fear of not belonging, came when I gave birth to my younger daughter at home in water. It was my dream birth and I think I needed to birth my baby exactly how I wanted to in order to forgive, let go of my anger, and move on past the fact that I was adopted. Birth is such a powerful thing, and for so many years I questioned how my birth mom could have given birth to me and maybe even held me and then given me away. And it wasn't until I gave birth in my own way that my vision of my own birth changed. Whatever the circumstances were when my mother birthed me, whether she held me or whether she was able to breastfeed me, I do know without a doubt that she did whatever she did with love. She gave me life. It's a lot.

For a long time, I still felt that I hadn't been loved during the time between my birth and my adoption, and that feeling of being unlovable stayed with me for so long. I was afraid of never being good enough and just had this crazy desire to be accepted. Shortly after my parents adopted me, a friend of theirs who was a nurse came over to our house and told my mom, "My gosh, Diane, I've held this baby before. My neighbor was a foster mother and this baby was at her house." And then she said to my Mom, "Just know that she was loved." Knowing that my mother's friend said that I was loved was comforting. It doesn't go any deeper than that. So I'm sure I was loved, but it's not the same as feeling like I belonged.

I've finally recognized that my adoption both does and does not define me. It's a part of who I am, but it doesn't have to control my decisions. Although I do feel like a lot of my fears as a child *have* affected my parenting. I want my own girls to know how connected I feel with them because I know what it feels like not to have that connectedness. I comfort them. I never let them cry it out. Part of it is because I believe in the attachment parenting model, but I also think it has a lot to do with wondering what happened to me in those first few months of my life. What happened to me between the time I was born and when I went to live with my parents, in that crucial infant stage, where I cried for the breast and milk and comfort and love? I have no idea.

When I held my first baby and saw how much she needed these things, I felt horrible because that's when I first realized what I *hadn't* gotten when I was born. It's hard to find a word to describe that emptiness. I know it stayed with me for so long, and I felt unlovable and not good enough and just this crazy desire to be accepted.

I know now that being adopted is something that happened to me and it's a part of who I am. Denying it for so many years wasn't healthy. I never want to live in denial like that again. I think part of me was afraid that by talking about my adoption, I would hurt my parents. Even though they always told me that if I wanted to talk about it or seek answers, they'd support me. I'll be 41 soon, and it's taken me a long time to get to a place where I can embrace this part of myself.

I've learned through my life that fear is an obstacle. We learn to be fearful. And we get to decide if we keep the obstacle in place or blast it down and overcome our fears. Fearlessness is living free and true and with pure enjoyment. We are all built to overcome fears and live free and true, but somehow we learn to feel afraid, inadequate or unworthy of happiness. Tearing down these walls of fear will bring bright days, fulfilled dreams and overflowing hearts. We just have to decide to be fearless.

∞

It's easy to explain away the emotion that comes with wanting to belong to this group or needing to feel love from that person. But as we can see from Anne's story, and from the other stories in this chapter, our need for love and belonging is such an integral part of who we are.

So when we feel that strong need to belong or to be loved, it's helpful to know our feelings are valid and are deeply connected to who we are and how we navigate our place in the world. At the same time, just because we all have these needs and the fears that go with them, we don't have to let them control the choices we make and our outlook on life. What's important is how we deal with these fears, because ultimately our choices may determine whether we live in fear or walk in freedom. And as we'll see in the chapters that follow, no matter where our fears come from, we have more power than we might have thought to work through them and even overcome them.

CHAPTER

4

IN THE BEGINNING, WE WERE FEARLESS:FINDING OUT HOW AND WHEN WE LEARNED TO FEAR

Love is what we were born with.
Fear is what we learned here.

– Marianne Williamson

Once upon a time, most of us were not so afraid to try new things or to dream. But somewhere, in between those first tender beats of our hearts and the vastness of our here and now, we learned to fear. In order to identify the root fears that keep us stuck, we have to be able to take a trip back to the beginning and get a good look at how and when we learned to fear in the first place.

Lessons of a Toddler

Have you ever just sat back and watched a toddler for a bit? If you haven't, then the next time you're out and about and there's a young child around, just stop and enjoy a little bit of tiny people watching. When we take the time to closely observe how a young child gets lost in her own little world, it's amazing to see how few boundaries she really has. Everything is new and exciting. She's ready to learn new things, venture into the unknown, and take on the world.

For the sake of illustrating this fearlessness, I'm going to share a bit about my own little 4-year-old, Jacq Jacq (Jacqueline). This little girl knows no limits or boundaries. At a young age, she could name off virtually every item on the top shelf of the pantry and leave us wondering *how* she knew this in the first place. She would climb up counters, cabinets and shelves. She would walk down the aisle of the grocery store singing her favorite song. You see, my little Jacq Jacq has very little fear.

Jacq Jacq is resilient. She'll run fast, fall down and scrape her knee, recover, then get back up and start running again. She's not afraid to try something new, fail, and then try again until she succeeds. She's not worried about hurting herself again after the fall. She takes what's happened, learns, and then jumps right back in.

She is adventurous. When we're in the grocery story, she'll wave and smile at everyone she sees without a second thought. She'll walk right up and talk to a stranger. She'll try new things, climb kitchen furniture and even attempt to wander out of the house to see what adventure lies beyond the front door if she can manage it.

Jacq Jacq is *very* persistent. You can tell her no what seems like a million times, and she'll keep coming back, "Please, mama? Please?" She's not afraid to ask again and again until I'm ready to either give in or have my head explode.

She easily forgives. Almost every time I admonish my little Jacq Jacq for some sort of wrong doing, she immediately flings herself into my arms demanding that we hug and make up. When she's sure that we're back to normal, she moves right along to her next bit of mischief.

Jacq Jacq is enthusiastic. She puts everything she has into everything she does. She'll start belting out her own made-up song wherever we are without a care in the world. She's not worried about what anyone around her is thinking or doing. She's free to be her enthusiastic, fearless self.

So looking at the fearless heart of a toddler, like Jacq Jacq, we might stop and think: "What the heck happened?" How did we go from being free to dream and believe in happy endings, to being afraid to even *talk* about our dreams, let alone try to go after them? When did we stop being so resilient and suddenly become terrified of getting hurt? When did failure become so big of a barrier that it completely blinded us to what might lie beyond? When did we stop forgiving? When did we start shutting others out? What happened to our never-ending persistence? Seriously. *What happened?*

Fear and Boundary-Setting

It all starts at the beginning, in our early childhood, with a mixture of building boundaries and suffering consequences. The way we approach fear as we grow is often affected by how we learned *to* fear as young children. We've already talked about how fear can help keep us safe, so let's now take a look at how a healthy connection between fear and safety can quickly morph into an unhealthy one that keeps us from moving forward.

A great way to define *healthy fear* would be to use the word "boundary" instead of the word "fear." Young children have to learn which boundaries will help them navigate through life without putting themselves in immediate danger. As we discussed in the first section of this book, there are certain boundaries that keep us safe and even help us to survive. It's how our boundaries are created when we're young that can make a huge difference in how we fear as we grow and how we see, or fail to see, these boundaries for what they really are - a way to keep us safe.

A toddler is so adventurous that she'll try new things without giving them a second thought. It's when she falls off the cabinet or hits the floor when she's running that she begins to learn to be afraid. These fear lessons are closely tied with how the people around her respond to her fall and can affect the way she reacts in similar situations as she grows.

Imagine that a toddler climbs up the kitchen cabinets when no one is watching, falls off, and hits the ground. Her mom makes a big fuss, and the toddler immediately begins to scream while her mom asks if she's okay and holds on to her for dear life. In this case, the child learns that if Mom is worried, then *she* should be worried. Insert fear. The next time she falls she'll be inclined to start panicking, and she might even think twice before being that adventurous again.

Let's take this same scenario, but switch it up a bit. The toddler falls. Mom watches anxiously, but waits to react. Her little girl whimpers for a second. Mom takes a deep breath, gives her a big hug, and reassures her that she's going to be okay before letting her know that maybe she shouldn't do that again. The toddler dusts herself off and moves on to the next thing. Insert *healthy boundary* instead of *fear*.

Looking at the connection between how we learn to fear and the lessons we learn in childhood can make us wonder about the degree to which adults feel like they were born fearless and the degree to which they believe their fearlessness is a result of how they were raised. In our next story, we'll see where Brittany believes her own fearlessness came from and whether she thinks it's because of how she was born, raised, or a combination of both.

∞

I'VE NEVER REALLY BEEN AFRAID OF THINGS BECAUSE I WAS RAISED TO BELIEVE I'M COMPLETELY LOVED, ADORED AND COMFORTABLE IN THE LIFE MY FAMILY HAS GIVEN ME AND WHAT THEY'VE HELPED TO ME ACHIEVE. I KNOW THAT I AM LOVED AND SUPPORTED. THAT'S NEVER BEEN A QUESTION.

- BRITTANY

Brittany is a 32-year-old morning news anchor and managing editor for Good Day Columbia. She loves to spend time with her family and friends, travel and cook.

I'm not really self-conscious. I'm a pretty secure person and always have been. I've never been scared of spiders or snakes. You'll find a picture on Facebook where I have a tarantula on top of my head when on a live shoot in Indiana. I'll try anything. I'll eat anything.

I've never really been afraid of things because I was raised to believe I'm completely loved, adored and comfortable in the life my family has given me and what they've helped me to achieve. I know that I am loved and supported. That's never been a question. I'm also naturally wired this way. My brother and I are different in many ways but he also has the same sense of confidence and drive.

My parents were the "you're fine" parents. When we fell, they used to tell us to just hop back up and that we were fine. They always gave us free range to be who we were. I was a really good kid, so I rarely got punished and when I did do something wrong my parents would sit down with me and logically talk through whatever had happened: "Why did you do this? Why do you think we're upset with you? Why is this a problem?" They taught us to be very logical and to think things through.

Thinking logically isn't always easy, especially when emotion is present. I love the quote "The heart has reason of which reason knows nothing." I am an emotional person and I'm totally aware of that. That's why it's very important to me to separate logic and emotion and to get to the point where I don't even do it consciously. My parents taught my brother and me to logically think through situations, so I'm able to question why I would be scared of certain things that I know logically present no real danger. For example, if a snake is poisonous and I'm afraid to hold it, that's a logical fear because I know it can hurt me. Or if I'm afraid to eat something new and strange because it might make me sick, there's a logical fear there too.

I think most fear is irrational and usually connected to something else at a deeper level. A lot of times, fear is connected to emotion and if you can just separate the two then you can overcome your fear.

∾

Brittany's story shows us that we learn a lot about what and how to fear from what we see in the world around us and how we're treated by those closest to us every day. And the innate fearlessness that many of us have when we're really little can either be built up or torn down as we grow, whether it's through an adult in our lives or by being the victim of childhood or adolescent bullying.

Let's take the persistence of a child who asks incessantly for cookies, her mom calmly tells her daughter that "no means no" and the child stops asking. The child hopefully learns healthy boundaries that will eventually help her to discern when it's time to be persistent and when it's time to back down.

On the other hand, when a child asks and asks and - as a result - is yelled at, demeaned, and told to "shut up and stop asking," she can begin to think her mom's anger is a direct reflection of herself, instead of her behavior. Perhaps she learns that she shouldn't have asked for what she wanted in the first place. Perhaps she begins to be afraid to ask for what she *needs* moving forward, because she's learned to fear the consequences of being persistent.

Instead of being taught the importance of healthy boundaries, she's already feeling that sense of being unworthy or unlovable as a direct result of asking for what she wants or needs. Therefore, persisting in this case - at the deepest level - has taught her that it could mean risking love.

So, *when* did we stop being so resilient? *When* did failure become that big of a barrier? *When* did we stop forgiving? *When* did we start shutting others out? What happened to our never-ending persistence?

Our negative childhood experiences, such as the one depicted above, can gradually strip us of the ability to be wholehearted and fearless. As children, we don't know how to cure or deal with this pain, so we put a band-aid over it and move on as best we know how. We build our walls so high and so thick with the bricks we create from our fears along the way, and eventually we forget how or why each brick was put there in the first place.

Fear and Abuse

It's one thing to have a tough life, where perhaps we weren't given all of the advantages that others may have had. But when we're abused – emotionally, physically, sexually – we are gradually stripped of both the second and third levels of safety that Maslow describes – the need for security of body, as well as the need for love and belonging. And anytime we're feeling unsafe, we're also feeling fear.

So we may have been born fearless, but when we're abused, we are essentially being told or shown that we are *not worthy* of being respected. We are *not worthy* of being loved. And when we're treated with this lack of dignity, we can actually begin to believe it and become afraid that perhaps we are unlovable after all, perhaps we really *don't* belong. And how can we trust and continue to move forward when we're feeling this way, struggling with feelings of being unlovable, unworthy and ashamed?

It would be easy to think that abuse isn't as common as it is because we don't openly talk about it. We're often afraid to speak out against abuse, and this silence can magnify the shame that victims may already feel. When society as a whole tends to sweep the issue of abuse under the rug, it can create an environment in which the fears of being unlovable and unworthy start to run the show and we find our fear boundaries shrinking, affecting many areas of our lives. We can see this in the next story, where we'll learn from Kiara the deep connection between the abuse she faced and the fears that remained for years following her abuse.

∞

TO ME, FEAR IS NOT BEING WORTHY. NEVER BEING GOOD ENOUGH. THEY SAY HINDSIGHT IS 20/20, AND AS I BEGAN TO HEAL, IT BECAME EASY TO SEE THAT

THE TRUST THAT WAS BROKEN SO MANY YEARS AGO HAD BUILT THIS HUGE WALL AROUND MY HEART THAT I HAD SPENT SO LONG DENYING WAS EVEN THERE. I HAD THIS OVERWHELMING FEAR THAT I WOULD NEVER BE "GOOD ENOUGH."

- KIARA

Kiara is a 34-year-old computer technician who has been married for five years and enjoys shopping, traveling and spending time in her garden.

Perhaps it is because I was in the middle of a large family with so many children. Perhaps it is because my parents spent a lot of emotional energy outside the home. Perhaps it is because of a rough upbringing. But beginning with some of my earliest memories, I had this innate desire to feel special. All I wanted was to know that I was completely cherished and loved for who I was, but I often felt lost between very talented older siblings, needy younger siblings and a mom who was often stretched, "gived out" and tired.

I grew up in a very isolated community in the middle of nowhere. I was homeschooled at a time where there were no active local homeschool groups. I had no close friends to call my own. As a strong-headed young girl, I didn't really connect with my siblings either. I often fought with my immediate older sister and was unable to really relate to my younger siblings. I desperately wanted to feel loved and special, so when a family friend came around and made me feel wanted, that's exactly how I felt - special. What began as him giving me little gifts and trinkets that made me feel special quickly crossed the line into sexual abuse.

I think it was my paralyzing fear of being unlovable and unwanted as a child, further compounded by this abuse, that has affected so much of my life. My ability to love. My ability to allow myself to be loved. My ability to understand what love truly is, my ability to let someone in, and my ability to quickly shut someone out.

As a teenager and young woman, having been so deeply affected by my past abuse, I would equate being physically desired with being loved. So even though I *knew* that true love went so much deeper than a physical relationship, I still found myself seeking that kind of attention, because I so desperately wanted to be loved, and when I felt *wanted* I also felt loved.

But as a married woman, I found the opposite to be true. I found that I could easily give myself physically, but when it came to opening my heart and truly letting my spouse in, at times that seemed virtually impossible. I found that the connection between my heart and body seemed to have been shattered. I went from thinking that being physically desired meant that I was lovable to being able to give my body, and yet hold back my heart.

To me, fear is not being worthy. Never being good enough. They say hindsight is 20/20, and as I began to heal, it became easy to see that the trust that was broken so many years ago had built this huge wall around my heart that I had spent so long denying was even there. I had this overwhelming fear that I would never be "good enough." It's only years later that this wall has finally begun to crumble.

∞

Kiara's experience is just another lesson in how the extreme hurts we experience in life can dig some deep roots, causing us to build walls that stop us from loving completely and being fearless. When we look at the statistics on abuse, it's clear just how common abuse is in our society. According to the National Center for Victims of Crime, one in five girls in the United States is a victim of sexual abuse. Safe Horizon notes that one in four women will experience domestic violence in her lifetime, and the National Institute of Justice and Centers for Disease Control and Prevention found that one in six women has been the victim of an attempted or completed rape.

So looking at the statistics on abuse alone, we can deduce that for many of us our deepest fears of rejection and unworthiness are rooted in some type of abuse - be it emotional, physical or sexual - that we have suffered as children or even adults. And because these fears run so deep, we build our fear boundaries especially high and strong when they're connected to abuse, making it that much harder to break through them in the end.

In our next story, we see how Teri's fears manifested in her life in the years after being raped. Her story reminds us that we can find our way through our fears, even if they cut right to the core of how we live and love.

∞

I JUST KNOW THAT IF THERE'S ANY OTHER WOMAN OUT THERE WHO'S STRUGGLING WITH ALL THE FEARS IN THE AFTERMATH OF SOMETHING LIKE THIS, WELL, I JUST WANT TO GIVE HER SOME HOPE THAT IT'S POSSIBLE — EVEN ON DAYS WHEN IT SEEMS SO IMPOSSIBLE — TO WORK THROUGH ALL THE FEAR AND TO FIND YOURSELF AGAIN.

- TERI

Teri is a 37-year-old married mom of two. She has taught elementary school for 15 years and believes that one day soon she'll start speaking out publicly against rape.

I remember calling my best friend on the phone in tears. I couldn't even get out a sentence, so she just told me to come to her office right away. I don't even remember the 20-minute drive over there, but I do remember stumbling out of the car, sitting down on the curb outside of her office building, and just shaking and crying uncontrollably. I answered her questions through my tears. I had been raped. Yes, I knew the guy. No, I didn't call the police. No, I didn't go to the hospital. Yes, I had already showered and changed my clothes.

I had actually tried to go to work that morning as if nothing had happened, but about 30 minutes into the day I broke down and had to leave. I remember my best friend driving me to the hospital, but what unfolded over the next few hours was hard to process. I felt so alone when they made my friend stay in the waiting room. The rape kit they ran was awful and I remember just sitting there in that cold exam room with those horrible fluorescent lights buzzing above me for what felt like forever.

I remember that the nurse scolded me for taking a shower the night before, and for not coming to the hospital right away.

I felt like she treated me like I was stupid, but in the hours following the rape all I could think about was washing him off of me. I didn't care about anything else. And it was like I was operating outside my body. I was in complete shock, and this nurse's lack of compassion was like a knife in an already broken heart.

When the police officer came in to take the report, I wouldn't give him the name of the man who raped me, although I did know his name. And I just couldn't go along with the police officer's recommendation to press charges. In the moment, I was so afraid of what anyone would think of me if it all got out. I lived in a small town, was teaching elementary school, and had a kind of high-profile position in the community. I didn't want *anyone* to find out. I just wanted to disappear. I wanted it all to go away.

It didn't, of course, just go away. It never does. In the years that followed, I developed a deep fear of a lot of things that I had never been afraid of before – connecting with men, being intimate, someone finding out what had happened, him finding me and coming after me. So much confusion. So much pain. So much deep fear. I also started to do this thing which I'm sure is pretty common, but I don't know – I'm not a doctor – where my body, mind and heart just completely disconnected from each other. I had always been really connected intimately with the guys I had dated, and overnight it was like I developed this inability to connect at all.

It wasn't until I met my husband that I really knew that I wanted and needed to connect with someone on a deep level. This caused me to begin to process what had actually happened to me. To heal. It had honestly been so much easier to just let my fear paralyze me than to think about working through the mess.

It still affects me in some real ways, though. Intimacy for me is different than it was before I was raped. I can draw a clear line – before and after. And what's crazy is that the things I'm afraid of now are things that I was never afraid of before, and that honestly don't even make much sense. Like I'm afraid of rejection sometimes, of physically being rejected by my own husband, which is crazy because I *know* how much he loves me. That fear of rejection isn't rooted in anything real, but it's still there. And sometimes my fear just makes me so sad – like

I wish my husband knew who I was, and how I was, before I was raped. I don't want to get into too much detail here, but let's just say I had a fearlessness when it came to the physical side of things that I just don't have anymore. And it's sad that I gave that part of myself to guys who didn't deserve it and that my husband, who loves me so deeply, doesn't really get to see that part of who I am. It's like it left me. Maybe I'll get it back someday and I'll stop being so afraid. I don't know.

The rape was over a decade ago and talking about it now is still nearly impossible for me. I can't believe I've even shared all this with you. I guess I just know that if there's another woman out there who's struggling with all the fear in the aftermath of something like this, well, I just want to give her some hope that it's possible – even on days when it seems so impossible – to work through all the fear and to find yourself again. It's not easy, but it's possible. I'm still working on it, but I'm determined to not let the fear control this part of my life forever.

∞

When a woman is harassed, abused or raped, like we see with Teri, it's not something easy to talk about, even if she wants to, and often it's something she won't report, even when she knows that by reporting the crime she might save another possible victim. She's afraid she'll no longer be seen as the strong woman. The entrepreneur. The adventurer. The wonder woman she may have felt like she was before. No. Now she is a not only seen as a victim, but suddenly all her other titles cease to exist. She doesn't stand up for herself for fear of losing herself.

So in order to move forward, we have to take this opportunity to be completely honest with ourselves about our past without getting stuck there. We have to take a good look at the root fears that are still holding us captive, so we can work toward taking that next step to freedom.

Fear and Public Humiliation

Have you spent time in a classroom full of young children recently? Have you seen their enthusiasm? The way so many of them are so eager to raise their hands and answer questions? The fearlessness with which many of them approach the novelty of learning new things and figuring out the world around them?

Now fast forward ten years to when that same group of eager 5- and 6-year-olds are now teenagers. They're sitting in a high school class and now *nobody* wants to raise their hand. Their teacher asks a question and is met with only silence.

What happened to them? To us? When did we start becoming afraid to answer a question or stand out in a crowd? Somewhere between kindergarten and high school, a student raises her hand to ask a question and then is humiliated in front of the class for asking a "stupid" question. Immediately, she feels not only embarrassed, but alone, standing out like a sore thumb, feeling like she doesn't belong. She learns that if she doesn't want to feel this way, it would be better if she didn't ask any questions at all. Why risk standing out, sharing her thoughts, admitting that she even *has* a question if the result is going to be humiliation? Likewise, those who witness her humiliation also learn that unless they want to suffer the same consequences, they best stay silent.

This is what happened to Ann, who at the young age of 10 found herself being openly and publicly humiliated and bullied by her teacher. As we can see in how she defines fearlessness, her traumatic experience when she was a child *still* impacts her life in a powerful way.

∞

TO ME, FEARLESSNESS WOULD BE WALKING INTO A ROOM, RELAXED, WITH A SMILE ON YOUR FACE, KNOWING THAT YOU'RE GOING TO MEET PEOPLE WHERE THEY ARE AND INTERACT GENUINELY WITH THEM WITHOUT BARRIERS OF FEAR GETTING IN YOUR WAY.

- ANN

Ann is a 40-year-old homeschool mom. She plays the banjo in an Americana band and has been married for 17 years.

Going into fifth grade I was an outgoing, kind of eccentric child, who was creative and interested in pretty much everything. But when I started my fifth grade year, I had a teacher who seemed so miserable and acted like she hated her job. Looking back, I honestly think the way that she dealt with her own misery was by taking her frustrations out on a particular student. That year that student just happened to be me.

That whole school year, I lived with my teacher telling me that I was stupid, annoying and worthless. She would tell me that nobody liked me. And it didn't take long for the other 29 kids in my class to join her.

I remember this one day when the teacher brought granola bars to class and told us that if we did well on our tests, she would give us a treat. I was already hypersensitive to everything because she had begun humiliating me in front of the class when I made mistakes. She would tell the kids how my grades were dropping and how I was going to be kicked out of the gifted program. So when I did well on my test, the teacher gave me one of these granola bars. I opened it, took one bite, and couldn't stand the taste of it. It was a sticky granola bar, and the way it felt in my mouth reminded me of maggots moving. I immediately got up and threw it in the trash. I didn't raise my hand – I just went up and did it because I was trying to be quiet and inconspicuous. When I returned to my seat and my teacher saw that I didn't have my granola bar and everyone else had theirs, she started yelling at me in front of the class: "Oh my gosh! I can't believe you ate so fast! What's wrong with you? Why are you such a pig?" Of course the whole class turned and looked at me, snickering and making fun of me for being such a pig.

In that moment of humiliation all those years ago, I remember feeling like my stomach just dropped out of me. I knew what she said would be used against me, I knew that I was being humiliated and people were going to make fun of me for it. So it's one of those moments when you know your life is changing.

That year was earth-shattering for me. I was humiliated at school and then felt misunderstood when I went home and tried to explain what had happened to my parents. Sometimes I didn't have the words and other times they didn't believe me. Then, when they did start to believe me they said they couldn't do anything about it. They tried to get my class changed, but it was already too late in the school year. And since my dad was a teacher in the district and was trying to get tenure, he didn't want to make any waves.

I knew my parents loved me – there wasn't a doubt in my mind that they wouldn't do their best to help or protect me. Yet I still struggle with my relationship with my mom to this day because I feel like there were a few times when she threw me to the wolves. Where she didn't protect me, and I felt like I was abandoned.

She later told me that it was only a year, that I was over-exaggerating, that it couldn't possibly have been that bad. I think this is a poor lesson to teach any child – that it's okay to be abused, to just sit there and take abuse of any kind. The verbal abuse I suffered at the hands of my teacher and classmates that year did, in some ways, make me very fearful of life. I was afraid to talk to people, I was afraid to open up in the slightest way. I felt that anyone who saw any part of me would just use it against me and I'd be humiliated all over again.

As the years went on I'd still hear myself saying things like, "Why are you such a pig?" I know whose voice that is and I have to remind myself that it's not true, that the voice I hear is lying. It's been something that has taken me years to get over. Now I'm finally in a place where I'm not afraid of other people, not afraid to walk out in public or to be vulnerable in front of people. But it's taken me a long time to get here.

I feel like I've been able to overcome many of the things that have happened, but still there are times when I will hear that voice in my head telling me that I'm worthless and that nobody loves me. Somehow I learned that I've got to go through life everyday *with* people, because you can't come through life without socializing.

In some ways, there have been times in my life – because of what I experienced in fifth grade – when I have been a very fierce fighter for myself. I stood up against teachers in subsequent years. I listened to my conscience and defended my beliefs in situations where no one else was. And yet there are other times when I *haven't* stood up because of fear, when I haven't done the right thing because I got to the crossroads and just froze. And of course that's had a negative impact on my life.

As for how I now feel about that teacher, there are times when I'm in a forgiving place, and there are other times when I struggle with forgiveness. The emotional pain comes back to me sometimes when I feel that someone has made fun of me or has done something that puts me right back in that fifth grade class. And I'll get angry at that teacher all over again. It's these times when I have to remind myself that forgiveness is necessary. It's a spiritual mandate. If I'm ever going to be happy or be the best person I can be, I have to forgive. The forgiveness, of course, is for me, not her.

Because of my past, I would personally define fear as exclusion – being unable to connect to other people and being unable to feel like you're yourself and comfortable around others. To me, fearlessness would be being able to walk into a room, relaxed, with a smile on your face, knowing that you're going to meet people where they are and interact genuinely with them without barriers of fear getting in your way.

Now when I start to freeze up, I just remind myself that the only way for me to let go of my fear is to push through it. Otherwise, it's just going to grow bigger and bigger until I feel trapped. A part of moving forward in my life is facing fears. I don't think anyone *likes* to face fears, but that's the only way you can grow.

∾

The lesson we learn from Ann's story is how public humiliation can sometimes shape our inability to push ourselves outside of that area where we know we'll be safe. It's in this environment where we sometimes develop the very fears that we'll carry with us for years.

There are, however, those who are not only spared the experience of public humiliation in their early years, but are also lifted up by those closest to them so that when they do face obstacles in the world, they have a resilience and aren't afraid to step up and be heard. So when my daughter came home from school one day and shared the following story, it was a great reminder of how important it is to affirm our children so they feel confident in their own self worth.

∞

BRIGETTE, 12 YEARS OLD

I went to school one day and one of my friends said that she saw some girls laughing at my singing in church. Then at a sleepover soon after, she heard them gossiping again about my singing.

When I found out that those girls were talking about me, I realized they were just those kind of girls who like to gossip. I wasn't offended at all because it doesn't matter. It's not true. I've had a lot of compliments before and my mom tells me that I have a good voice.

When I think about those girls who talk about me that way, I think they must have hard lives because they need to put someone else down to make themselves feel better. It makes me feel sad for them.

∞

When Brigette came home that day and shared how these girls had been making fun of her, my blood immediately started to boil. The defender in me had to keep quiet as she explained what happened, because there was so much I *wanted* to say, but knew I shouldn't. When she finished sharing, I simply asked her, "How did that make you feel?" Her response was something like, "I'm fine. I just don't know if I should say something about it or not. What should I do?"

In a flash, my heart went from being defensive and upset for my "poor little girl" to feeling so proud of this young lady. The surety in her voice indicated that she was absolutely fine. Her self-esteem had not taken a hit, and she could see beyond the petty meanness to the probable pain on the other side. So we decided that she should just continue being nice and know that those girls were not really her friends.

In the end, whether we're deeply afraid of speaking up or speak up all the time without fear of what others think, many of us can probably relate to the connection between public humiliation and how we learn *to* fear. When we add in the traumas, hurt and other negative experiences in our lives, it's just one thing after another that takes aim at our self-confidence, our self-love, and – in many cases – our very core beliefs that we are even worthy of love and belonging.

The Past Doesn't Have to Define the Future

Looking at our past, we can see how easy it would be to let it define who we are today. It's easy to recognize how our hurts, humiliations and consistent fear lessons help to shape and mold us. They affect what we pursue, how we react in certain situations, how we are connected and care about the opinions of those around us, and how we speak to ourselves when no one is listening.

It's easy to walk past the bathroom, catch a glimpse of our reflection in the mirror, and in a quick moment, say something completely unkind to ourselves. Our first reaction to our own reflection might be more heartless than anything we would ever say to another soul, because of the fears rooted in our past.

So, our boundaries have been set, and in many cases, they are no longer the healthy boundaries that keep us from harming ourselves, but rather the boundaries that keep us from trying something new or following our dreams. It can take years or perhaps a particular event or an a-ha moment to help us break free of these boundaries and start breaking down the walls and truly living.

This is what happened to Janice when she woke up in a hospital bed at the young age of 17. Her story shows us that at some point we can make a decision to not let our past, and all the fears that we carry with us from our childhood experiences, determine where we'll go or what we'll do next. She shows how we can allow our fears of being unlovable and unworthy define us, or we can choose to see these fears as challenges to work through and overcome.

∞

I WAS BATTLING ALL THESE FEARS. FEARS THAT NOBODY CARED FOR ME. FEARS THAT NOBODY LOVED ME. I FELT LIKE I WAS NOTHING. I DID NOT MATTER, AND THERE WAS NO REASON FOR ME TO BE HERE, SO I DECIDED TO TAKE SOME PILLS.

- JANICE

Janice is a 56-year-old successful business owner who has been happily married for 33 years. She loves to take weekend trips with her girlfriends and credits her stepmom for helping to raise her into the woman she is today.

Most of my childhood was spent in and out of the foster care system. My parents divorced when I was a little over a year old and my dad won custody of me and my sister. Our mom was a serious alcoholic and when she was only 35 years old, she died of alcohol poisoning. At that time my Dad didn't know what to do with two girls so he put us with a family he knew, and that was our first experience in the foster care system. We moved in with this family when I was one-and-a-half, maybe two, and stayed there for four years. They put us in school and raised us as part of their family. They were good to us, but we weren't their kids.

When my Dad remarried and returned for us, he was drinking heavily and my older sister took the brunt of the abuse. Life was hard for us and one night, when I was 13 years old, I remember my stepmom having to stop my dad when he was beating my head against the bedpost. If it weren't for her, I don't know if I would have gotten out of that situation. Not too long after this happened, the welfare department stepped in and I went back into the foster care system.

I went through a really dark time through 11th and 12th grades after having been in and out of foster homes. I was battling all these fears. Fears that nobody cared for me. Fears that nobody loved me. I felt like I was nothing. I did not matter, and there was no reason for me to be here, so I decided to take some pills.

I woke up in the county hospital and saw a nurse beside my bed. "What the hell is wrong with you?" she asked me. I probably looked at her kind of funny, because she followed with "Do you *know* how beautiful you are? How *lucky* you are?" She went on and on about how beautiful I was, how much I had to give in this life, and was I even thinking about my future children.

This little Christian woman ran down a whole list. She said to me "You know, God left you here for a reason!" I looked at her funny again, which prompted her to say, "I mean that. You didn't die for a reason. God left you here for a reason. You still have stuff to finish." That's exactly what she said to me.

This was a turning point in my life, and I think the Lord was asking me, "What is wrong with you? These people don't matter, you matter." That was my a-ha moment. I was 17.

That's when I stopped caring about the opinions of others. I decided that I was done being on welfare. I worked three jobs, got an apartment of my own, and paid my own rent.

Ever since then, my life has been blessed. The Lord has blessed me with a wonderful husband and a wonderful family, and the blessings keep coming. As far as my father and my past, all the hatred I had toward my father dissolved years ago when I realized that alcoholism is a true sickness. So I forgave him, because if we don't have forgiveness we can never move on.

Sometimes I get emotional. I used to ask God all the time, and I'm sure God is tired of me asking, "Why am I so blessed? Is what I went through as a child, the hard times, is that the reason why I'm so blessed?" I came from having nothing, to being able to buy whatever I want, whenever I want to. Giving has always been important to me, and I have been blessed to be able to help others. And when everything is given in the right heart, it always comes back to me tenfold.

∞

As we've seen throughout this chapter, the way we were treated as children strongly affects whether we become more fearful or fearless as we grow. Janice had a lot of fear. She didn't feel lovable or wanted and didn't have any strong models of fearlessness in her life when she was young. It was only after she woke up in the hospital, lucky to even be alive, that she stopped caring about the opinions of others and turned her life around.

Janice didn't have the encouragement that Madeline, who we feature in our next story, had from her parents. As we'll learn from Madeline's story, from the time that she was little her parents encouraged her and told her that she could do anything she set her mind to doing. So when she faced her biggest fear she had a solid foundation and many tools to help her work through it and overcome.

∞

EVEN THOUGH SOMETHING HORRIBLE HAPPENED IN MY LIFE, AND I KNEW IT WAS GOING TO BE HARD FOR ME TO OVERCOME, I WAS GOING TO HAVE TO LOOK AT THIS THE BEST WAY THAT I POSSIBLY COULD AND HOPEFULLY USE IT TO INSTILL IN OTHERS THAT YOU CAN DO ANYTHING THAT YOU SET YOUR MIND TO DOING IF YOU JUST BELIEVE IN YOURSELF.

- MADELINE

Madeline is a 27-year-old mother with a background in elementary education who is passionate about speaking to women and children about living fearlessly. She was attending college at the University of Alabama and preparing for the Miss Alabama USA Pageant when she was involved in a debilitating car accident.

My parents have always been very supportive and helped me get through hard times. They've always let me know that no matter what obstacles come my way, no matter what adversity I'm faced with, I can always push forward and fulfill my dreams. So when I had my accident, I know this is what helped me to overcome the many challenges and fears I faced in the days, months and years following.

One day, I was driving home from college when a deer ran

out in front of my car. I hit the deer, lost control, and drove off a 30-foot ravine. The car instantly caught on fire and I think I would have burned to death if it hadn't been for a truck driver who saw the accident. I was barely conscious, hanging upside down by my seatbelt and could barely speak or breathe, but remember him telling me, "Honey, we're going to get you out of here as quickly as we can."

As I was hanging there, my parents, my family, everything was just flashing before me like this could be it. So I remember saying a prayer that I would make it through this and somehow be able to inspire others.

The truck driver called 911 and I ended up being airlifted to the hospital. The next thing I remember is waking up from a coma 12 days later in the ICU. I was terrified. I had shattered my femur in 12 places, broken both bones in my right arm, broken all of my ribs on my left side, and had numerous internal injuries, including punctured lungs and a laceration in my liver. The doctors told my parents that they didn't know if I was going to be able to walk again. They said they might have to amputate my leg because it was shattered and they didn't know if they could do surgery right away because I had caught pneumonia.

I remember the first person I saw when I woke up was my dad. He was standing over my head and I just asked him, "Is everything going to be okay?" He told me yes. And I know this might seem crazy, but then I asked him, "Am I going to be able to compete in the Miss Alabama USA Pageant?" And he was like, "Oh no, honey. Not this year."

I was so scared because I didn't know where my life was going to go from there or what my next steps were going to be, but I knew that in order to overcome this I needed to surround myself with people who believed in me. I knew that somehow I would to be able to get back on my feet, return to college, finish my education, and compete in pageants again. I thought to myself, "I'm going to have to make sure that I turn this into something that can be good."

My dad always told me, "You can do anything that you set your mind to doing. You just have to believe in yourself and go for it." And this is what he told me after the accident. "You can still do whatever you want to do, even though you've had this happen.

You just have to believe in yourself and the sky's the limit."

Three tenets I've always lived by are: You've got to work hard. You've got to be persistent. And you've got to stay positive. That goes hand in hand with surrounding yourself with people that believe the same things. One of my favorite quotes is "Never let the fear of striking out keep you from playing the game." And that's one thing that I've always kept in the back of my mind and shared with others. You can't be fearful. You can't let fear get in the way of fulfilling your dreams and going after what you want in life.

I was in the hospital for about 23 days, and in a wheelchair for three months and basically confined to the house once I returned home. I had to teach myself how to walk again, with the help of a lot of in-home and then outpatient therapy. I couldn't do anything for myself. I couldn't bathe by myself. I couldn't go to the restroom by myself. I couldn't get anything to eat when I was hungry.

I was very depressed. Family and friends would come over to encourage me. And even though I had all these people telling me that I *could* do something and that I was going to be fine, at the end of the day I had to believe in myself and know that I could do it. A lot of people told me that I was never going to be able to compete in pageants again or do other things I had dreamed of. It was hard to get back up, but I just had to keep reminding myself that I could do anything that I set my mind to doing. I just had to believe in myself and put God first. My faith has helped me through a lot of things.

At the time of the accident, I had been preparing for Miss Alabama USA, so when it came time for the pageant, I decided to go watch the event in my wheelchair. I had over 30 scars on my body and usually in a pageant, they're like, "Oh! I need to cover this little tiny scar." So I felt like everyone was looking at me with pity and I even remember some people saying, "Oh, she'll never be able to compete again." But competing in the Miss USA Pageant was something I had always wanted to do, so I told my mom, "Next year, I want to be up on that stage and I want to compete."

In 2009, just a year after my accident, I competed for Miss Alabama USA and made the top ten. I told my mom I wasn't going to give up and that I wanted to compete again. The following year, I entered the pageant again and remember the girls saying stuff to me like, "Oh you have 30 scars?" I'm pretty sure they felt sorry for me, and I think they thought that I wasn't going to be able to win, but they were wrong. I won!

After I got married, I decided that I wanted to compete for Mrs. Alabama because I wanted to keep encouraging women and inspiring them to never give up. So I competed for Mrs. Alabama in March and I won. Then I won Mrs. America in September and went on to compete in Mrs. World.

By the time I competed for Mrs. America, I had come to believe that dreams really are possibilities and that no matter what someone tells you, you can fight through and can fulfill your dreams. I've always had a passion for helping children, and after winning these pageants I have been able to use my platform to speak to both girls and women about the importance of never giving up and of not letting your fears and what you have been through in the past define you.

Because I had so many people tell me that I *couldn't* when I was *able*, and because I also had people like my parents who always told me what I *could* do, I am very passionate now about being a positive influence in the lives of others. I just want to be able to help change the way people believe, because a lot of people may be faced with hurdles in their lives that they think they can't get over. I want to help them see what's possible.

By the time I got to the Mrs. America pageant, I knew that with my faith, staying positive and believing in *me*, it didn't matter what anyone else thought. Win or lose, if I give 110% I'm going to be successful. I am here because I want to be able to help people who are fearful and instill in them that no matter what may come their way, they can do it. I pray – day in and day out – for the opportunity to use my story to help others. After I won the Mrs. America pageant, I knew going into the Mrs. World pageant that whatever was supposed to happen was going to happen, and that win or lose I was still going to be able to share my story and hopefully inspire others to not give up and to push forward no matter what adversity or obstacle may come their way.

∞

Both Janice's and Madeline's stories are examples of how our past plays a huge role in our present and our future and how we approach fear as we grow. We can take these lessons, whether positive or negative, and learn from them. If we had a hard past, like Janice, we can choose to break the cycle and leave a different legacy for our own children than was left to us. Or if we had parents or other adults in our lives who taught us what is possible, we can use the strength we gained from our childhoods to not only overcome tremendous obstacles – like Madeline did – but to also pay it forward. Regardless of our past and whether our childhood influences look more like Janice's or Madeline's or somewhere in between, we *can* look towards our future with fearlessness and hope.

CHAPTER

5

A TISKET, A TASKET, FEAR IN MY BASKET: HOW FEAR MANIFESTS ITSELF IN OUR DAILY LIVES

∞

There are four ways you can handle fear. You can go over it, under it, or around it. But if you are ever to put fear behind you, you must walk straight through it. Once you put fear behind you, leave it there.

– Donna Favors

Now that we know what fear is and where it comes from, we can dive into how fear manifests itself in our daily lives and why it often has this invisible control over many of our everyday decisions and actions. Looking at the difference between the adventurous toddler and the cautious adult, we can easily see that the way fear shows up is closely tied to how we were raised and schooled and the life situations that we experienced between then and now.

Because of the hurt we have experienced, we learn that we

can't let people in as easily. Or that if we take a moment of boldness and just go for it, we might be humiliated. Unlike the young child who fails, learns and consistently tries again and again, over time we seem to adopt this concept that failure is bad.

Fears slowly creep into our lives and begin to form a boundary. Inside the boundary is where we feel safe or comfortable. If we're going to try something new, if we're going to go after that big goal or dream, we have to be able to break through this boundary. In order to do this we have to face our fears because each brick of this wall is made up of them. You see, *it is fear that defines the boundaries of our comfort zone.*

Sometimes stepping outside of our comfort zone, as we'll learn with Tierica's story, can define for us what it means to be able to name our fears so that we can clearly claim them and walk through them. Even though Tierica had spent a lot of time on stage before the moment she describes in her story, she still had to choose - in a moment of real fear - to either step up to the plate or not. She chose to step up, and the lives she impacted that day through her words marked a powerful moment of growth in her life.

∞

HE HANDED ME THE MIC AND I WAS REALLY SCARED. THE VERY SILENCE THAT I WAS SUPPOSED TO FILL CONSUMED ME WITH FEAR.

- TIERICA

Tierica is a 28-year-old entrepreneur, author and spoken word artist who empowers young women and educators throughout the country through trainings, workshops and writing.

One of the things that I do to help with fear is to make sure that I'm prepared. To control what I *can* control and then practice what to do when things are out of control. So when I'm standing toe-to-toe with my fear, I can push through it and work to get the desired results.

I was working at an educational conference last year when my colleague, who was on stage giving a keynote speech, said, "Tierica. Come up here." When I first heard my name, I was okay because I'm a spoken word artist and used to being in front of people. But in this instance, I quickly became afraid. Knowing my colleague, he could have asked me to do anything. I could have been on my head breakdancing, there was no telling. So not knowing gave me fear.

I got up on stage and my colleague introduced me: "She's a spoken word artist out of Atlanta, Georgia. She's one of the most phenomenal spoken word artists in the country." Then he turned to me and said, "Tierica, give them ten seconds." Boom. He handed me the mic. And I was really scared. The very silence that I was supposed to fill consumed me with fear. As long as he was talking, I was okay.

So here I was, standing toe-to-toe with fear and my head was spinning with a million reasons why I should *not* do a poem. I was like, "I don't have a poem that's 10 seconds. Ok, Tierica, then give them 30 seconds. Which one should I do? Which poem should I do? Ok, I'll do this one - no, that won't be suitable for this audience or environment." So now all of these thoughts were racing through my head, and I had to tell myself, "You know what Tierica? You're scared." My heart was beating out of my chest, but I knew that I just had to do it. So I let it go and delivered a poem. And after I finished, everyone stood up and started clapping. That day I sold out of my poetry books.

I think that it's okay to be afraid. It's a necessity that lets you know that you're alive. It's not about promoting fear, but about focusing your attention more on what you do when you're afraid than on the fear itself.

∞

If we let them, all those "I can't do its" that fire off in our brains can turn into excuses that we use to avoid facing the discomfort of approaching our fear boundaries. But like we saw with Tierica, when we are able to name our fear and claim it for what it is, we can then move to the other side of it. Sometimes we can even do this in the very moment when we're feeling most afraid - of failure, of rejection, of being unlovable, of being humiliated - and move through this fear rather quickly.

How Fear Keeps Us From Making Decisions

The deep hidden roots of our fear become visible everywhere when we put on some fresh glasses and take a clear look around. Have you ever been hesitant to make a simple decision? The decision could be as small as introducing yourself to a new person, inviting someone over for coffee, deciding what dress to wear, or sharing a new idea at the company meeting. Take for example the simple question of "Where do you want to eat?" Do you ever counter with something like "I don't know, where do *you* want to eat?" and then go back and forth until a decision is finally made?

We could be afraid to decide which curtains to put on the windows, which gift to give a friend, which outfit to purchase. Essentially these decisions leave us with a question: Did I get the *right* curtains, outfit or gift? Maybe we wanted the really crazy-looking outfit, but we chose more conservatively because we were afraid of being judged on our choice. So we ask our friends, "What do you think?"

Do you ever just stop and ask yourself – Why does it matter? Do *you* like the curtains? Do *you* like the outfit? That should be the only question you need to answer. But we often have this desire to belong, so we make choices that we feel are acceptable to those around us. We find ourselves constantly second-guessing ourselves when instead perhaps we should be asking, "Why do I care?"

Fear and Comparison

These root fears often spill over into comparing ourselves to others. "They have a much nicer house than we do! She always has it so together. How does she do that? Look at those crafts! How fun! I wish I did those things with my kids. Look at how successful she is. Look who just got the new promotion at the office. What did I do wrong?"

It's so easy to look at those around us and immediately see what it is we *don't* have or we *aren't* doing. When we really think about it, where does comparison come from anyway? Why is it that if we don't have a perfect house, a homemade dinner on the table every night, an amazing job, you name it, we fall into that trap of feeling as though we are not enough? Seriously, what's going on here?

Honestly, it's often because we live in a society where it seems there never *is* enough. We're always wanting more. If we don't have this or that, we're often afraid we won't fit in – that we won't belong. It kind of takes us all the way back to high school, doesn't it? We find ourselves trying to be like or connect with the popular kids, it's just in a more adult setting. And if we *are* the popular kids, we want to figure out how we're going to keep up our perfect facade and not lose face. It's often hard to find contentment when we feel we don't measure up. When we take a closer look and ask ourselves why we care so much about the opinions of others, we often find that we're actually dealing with the fear of rejection that is closely connected to our need for love and belonging.

Fear of Rejection

Fear of rejection shows up in our daily lives in many ways. It can keep us from letting another person know that we truly love him or her. It can keep us from making new friendships and connections. It can keep us from joining a particular group we've been wanting to join. It's a fear that runs so deep that it can keep us from truly living and dreaming.

Adding to the complicated nature of fear, the fear of rejection is often compounded by the fear of being unlovable. If true love is found on the other side of our fear boundary, then we have to be able to navigate through and let go of our fears in order to find the value, self-worth and love that we seek. And we have to be able to let down our walls in order to let someone else in, which is what we'll learn from Bernadette's story about the fears of rejection she faced when she first started dating her now-husband.

∞

IT HAS TAKEN YEARS, A LOT OF BROKENNESS, HURT, FIGHTING, MAKING UP AND FORGIVING TO GET TO THE POINT WHERE MY HEART IS TRULY OPEN AND TRULY HIS. BUT THAT FEAR OF BEING REJECTED, OF NOT BEING GOOD ENOUGH, OF NOT BEING WORTHY OF TRUE LOVE EMOTIONALLY PARALYZED ME.

- BERNADETTE

Bernadette is a stay-at-home mom who has been married for 15 years and is actively involved in her local soccer community with her husband and children.

Aaron was my first real boyfriend. Oh, I had hung out with guys, made out with a handful or two, and had plenty of offers come and go over the years, but when it came to actually dating someone, I *knew* that I could only date someone who I could see myself marrying.

I remember at a college talent show belting out the song lyric, "When I give my heart, it will be completely, or I'll never give my heart." And I distinctly remember the intensity with which I felt and embraced this concept. I was literally *terrified* of getting hurt. I had been through so much hurt and rejection in my life already. Not feeling good enough. Not feeling *worthy* of truly being loved. Because of my difficult and somewhat isolated childhood, I had so many hard social lessons to learn, which ended up, in several instances, with friends who I loved more than anything completely dropping me overnight. My fear was intense and real.

Aaron and I had been dating for two weeks when I felt it - sheer panic. Looking back, it's clear that I was subconsciously trying to sabotage our new relationship, but at the time I really didn't understand the full depth of that panic. When I first met Aaron, he was always wearing contacts, except for every once in awhile when he would wear these gold glasses with a bar across the top that I absolutely hated. I began to notice *every* time he put those glasses on, and I couldn't stand it. I'm smiling as I write this and chuckling a bit, because I remember having a conversation with my friend about Aaron's glasses, and how he seemed to be wearing them more often. I was irritated to the core and remember telling her that I just didn't think my relationship with Aaron was going to work. I then proceeded to get on the phone with him and found a way to again - subconsciously - instigate a fight. No, I didn't mention the glasses, but over the phone you can bet your bottom dollar that I could *see* him wearing them.

After we got off the phone, our relationship's future was not looking very good. For some odd reason, I was compelled to walk off campus and over to his house. Why? Honestly, I believe - and deep down, I believed this from the night of our first date - that Aaron and I are one of those couples who were just meant to be. So I feel God had a huge hand in what happened next. I walked up to Aaron's door, knocked, and when he opened it, there he was standing in the doorway with a broken pair of gold, wiry, ugly glasses dangling from his hand. Apparently, after he got off the phone with me, he accidentally sat on them - to my heart's delight! To this day, my friend swears that was a minor miracle that saved our relationship.

That's just one instance of many where my fear of rejection and being unlovable showed up in a seemingly unrelated way. Aaron and I were engaged for several months when our parish priest encouraged us to set some boundaries, since we were waiting until we were married to have sex. Following in the footsteps of my older sister, I suggested we cut out kissing and everything but holding hands until our wedding day. Believe me, that was *not* easy. But what I discovered in those six months was that my heart had still not been fully opened to this man. Because of my history of childhood abuse and because I always felt that guys never really cared about my heart, it took this six months with Aaron to truly fall in love. When making out, kissing, touching - when all of that was taken off the table - all we were left with was us. *That* was when our friendship started to blossom. *That* was when I began to truly open my heart to this man who loved me more than anyone had ever loved me before.

It has taken years, a lot of brokenness, hurt, fighting, making up and forgiving to get to the point to where my heart is truly open and truly his. But that fear of being rejected, of not being good enough, of not being worthy of true love emotionally paralyzed me. The walls were thick and tight, but bit by bit, were brought down by the greatest gift that my God has given to me, my husband. And yes, the first big chop at that huge wall began with a pair of broken glasses.

∞

We see in Bernadette's story how fear can show up and rob us of our peace and ability to open up our hearts and dream. Fear was given to us as a gift to help us navigate the world safely, but sometimes the very gift that should be helping to keep us safe actually holds us captive. This captivity becomes clear in Denise's story, where we see that when it comes to those we love, often the fears that cause us to protect our loved ones so fiercely in the first place can also keep us from fully living.

∞

I LIVED WITH FEAR THE ENTIRE TIME JOSH WAS GROWING UP. I WOULD NEVER LET HIM RIDE A MOTORCYCLE, NEVER LET HIM GO ANYWHERE THAT I THOUGHT MIGHT BE DANGEROUS. I WAS FEARFUL OF EVERYTHING. I WAS SCARED TO DEATH OF LOSS.

- DENISE

Denise is a 55-year-old wife, mother and veteran FedEx express employee. She lost both a disabled husband and a teenage son to death by suicide.

When I hear the word fear, the first word that comes to mind is death. I have a big fear of losing people in my life. I suffered the loss of both a husband and child, so I'm sure that's why when I think of fear I think of death first.

I had only been married nine months and was five months pregnant when my husband fell and broke his neck, becoming a quadriplegic. He had two kids from a previous marriage, so I found myself pregnant with a disabled husband and two children to care for, after having waited until I was 30 years old, happily married, and financially secure to even get pregnant. I had had my life planned out, so this was all very frightening.

When my husband had his accident, it was the first time I really began to fear - I had grown up in a good family and had had a great life up to this point. Now we had to sell everything we owned and move into my parents' house for what turned out to be a year and a half. When my husband broke his neck, the man I fell in love with and married became a different person. He needed around the clock care. It was very difficult. I can remember when he was in the hospital, and they were turning him side to side in intensive care. I remember thinking, "How could it possibly get any worse?" Then all of a sudden he couldn't breathe, and then he got pneumonia. And I think I learned right away to not allow myself to think that way. When you think things can't get any worse, they often do.

Once it seemed like our life was getting a little better, we decided to build our own home. A month after moving in, when Josh was 18 months old, my husband died by suicide.

My husband's death changed everything. I lived with fear the entire time Josh was growing up. I would never let him ride a motorcycle, never let him go anywhere that I thought might be dangerous. I was fearful of everything and scared to death of loss. Even though I grew up riding motorcycles my whole life, I still wouldn't let my son near them.

I was always afraid that something bad was going to happen to Josh. I feared someone was going to steal him from me when he was little, even when at the grocery store I was terrified that if I left him for a second, he'd be taken. My therapist told me my fears were so intense because I had already suffered so much loss.

By the time Josh was a teenager, I had moved on with my life, remarried, and had another child. Josh was in honors classes, ran track, had a lot of friends and even went on a couple of trips to Europe and China as part of a student ambassador program. The very furthest thought from my mind was that Josh would take his own life, so when he died by suicide it completely changed my whole outlook on fear.

I know it's natural for people to want to cast blame when someone dies, but what I learned after my husband's death is that we can't blame ourselves. Josh's death was nobody's fault. It was his choice and that was so clear in my mind because of what I had been through with my husband. Josh was only 18 months old when his Dad died by suicide, and he was legally adopted by my current husband, Steve, so he grew up in a loving family. There were no signs whatsoever that he might kill himself, which was the hardest thing for me. I never felt angry towards Josh – I just felt really badly that I never knew that anything was wrong.

When Josh died, a lot of my fear died with him because I realized that all those years, all the fears I had been hanging on to - fear of him getting on a motorcycle, fear of him or his brother getting hurt, fear that one or the other of them was going to break his neck - didn't even matter. I realized there are no guarantees in life. It changed everything for me.

I would get down on my knees everyday and beg God not to let me ruin my younger son Randy's life or my husband's life. I wanted to die, but I knew that I couldn't because I had other people I knew I needed to live for.

So I tried hard to give Randy as normal of a childhood as I could. He was only 11 when his brother died. When Randy turned 13, I bought him a dirt bike and he started racing motocross, if that gives you any indication of how I just let go of the fear. I was still worried that he might get hurt, but I learned you only live once and that was Randy's big dream, so I let him go for it. I never would have let Josh do that.

Randy is 20 years old now, and if anything happened to him I don't know what I would do. I have to block these thoughts out of my head because anything could happen at any time. I've been involved in support groups with mothers who have lost more than one child, so I know it's possible. Randy's been a pretty responsible kid, but once in awhile if I wake up in the middle of the night and he's not home yet, my mind goes to the "what ifs." But you can make yourself sick with fear that way, so I just try not to go there.

I hope that mothers reading this know that we just have to be the best moms we can for as long as we can, because we don't know how long our kids are going to be here with us. That's why when I see people waiting for the perfect time to do certain things, I always tell them that you can plan all you want, but life's going to turn out how it's going to turn out. It doesn't always work out. It just doesn't.

I'm grateful today for my husband and son, but I never thought my life would go quite this way. I never wanted just one child. I planned my kids. When we had Randy, we were a content family of four. Never in my wildest dreams did I think it would be just the three of us. So, you can try to plan your life all you want, but God's got His own plan.

All I can say now is that I'm a very faithful person. I read the Bible, go to church, and find peace in my spirituality with God. So living fearlessly means living my life one day at a time. I feel like I've been picking myself up and dusting myself off forever now. I'm not angry about any of it and I've let go a lot of that fear. And letting go of my fear feels good.

∞

As we discussed in Chapter One, our fear can guide us, keep us safe, and even warn us, "Don't go there! Don't do that!" And yet one of the lessons we learn from Denise's story is that even if our fear is grounded in a very real place, and even if we believe it's our fear that's keeping us and those we love safe, when it comes down to it, it's not usually our *fear* that's going to save us in the end.

When we look at our own lives and the way that fear shows up everyday, most of us – if we're willing to be honest with ourselves and do the work – can make the choice each and every day to *not* let fear rule the way we live our daily lives. This is true in the little fears we face, as well as the big fears. We just need to see where the roots of these fears are and be brave enough to face them head on.

PART II

OVERCOMING IT

∞

Inaction breeds doubt and fear.
Action breeds confidence and
courage. If you want to conquer
fear, do not sit home and think
about it. Go out and get busy.

– Dale Carnegie

CHAPTER

IT ALL STARTS WITH WHY: FINDING THE WHY THAT DRIVES US

The two most important days in your life are the day you were born and the day you find out why.

– Mark Twain

The old hymn "Amazing Grace" goes, "I once was lost, but now I'm found, was blind, but now I see." When we can finally *see*, it means there's *hope* because when we can see how our root fears manifest themselves in our lives, we *know* what we're looking for. We can take a good, clear look into our own hearts and say, "Wow! That is why I hurt!" or "That is why I feel nothing. This is what has been holding me back and why I've been unable to take the next step."

It's like turning the light on in a dark room with an intruder. When we can see, we can fight. We know what hits to dodge and what punches to throw. As we move into this next section, it's time to take those steps to finally shatter our fear boundary.

This is the part of our journey where we know what we have to work on and where we get to roll up our sleeves and just *get it done.* That sounds easy, doesn't it? Well, it's not necessarily going to be easy and I can't promise it will be fun, but it's in these final chapters that we're going to do the work to get to the other side of that fear boundary and find the freedom we've been seeking. And you know what? It all starts with WHY.

Have you ever asked yourself *why* you want to change? *Why* you want to reach that next goal or follow that dream? *Why* it even matters? The word why in and of itself might be small, but this one word can mean the difference between pushing through that fear boundary or deciding that it's just not worth it and staying where we feel most comfortable.

You see, our WHY is one thing unique to each of us that will drive us through the days when we just want to give up. It will help us through the days when everything feels as though it's falling apart. It will push us through the days when some shiny, new thing comes along, grabs our attention, and tries to pull us away from our goal. Our WHY will stop us, help us regain focus, and drive us onward. And it's this WHY that will allow us to build the bridge that will get us from the center of our comfort zone out into the great wild and beautiful land of living fearlessly.

Digging Into Our WHY

It's so much easier to *talk* about our dreams than it is to take action toward reaching them. Think about it - dreams can be so much fun, although sometimes scary, to talk about. We can envision the life we want so clearly, and there's an energy and excitement to the conversation. "Yes," we think, "we *really* want this!" We're ready to dive in, and we think we understand why. We make a plan and move forward full steam ahead. We commit ourselves to achieving our dreams and we're feeling great!

But here's what happens when we haven't really tapped into our WHY. We're all gung ho, excited and moving forward, until we get blindsided one day. Or we fail. Big time. The doubt and fear start to creep in, and we begin to second-guess ourselves and wonder if our dream is really that important in the first place. This fear begins to paralyze us and before we know it, we're right back to where we started, stuck in the middle of that safety zone, going nowhere.

The thing is, if we chase a dream without taking the time to dig into why we want it in the first place, then it's easy to give into our fears or convince ourselves that our dream really isn't that important after all. Other distractions start to steal our attention and we begin to think that we just might be better off jumping ship, moving in a different direction, or refocusing our energy elsewhere.

And yet if we are able to dig deeply into *why* we want to go after our dreams in the first place and can connect to our vision because we understand *why* we're making sacrifices, we'll be better equipped to dust ourselves off when we fall and stay focused when we get weary. This is when we know that our fear doesn't stand a chance. We're moving into the realm of fearlessness. And even though it isn't always easy, those walls start to break down as we make our way through our fear boundary, and it begins to feel a lot like freedom.

For some of us, our WHY will smack us in the face, so big and intense that it will push us through most any hardship. For others, our WHY might come as a more subtle series of events in our lives that gradually reveal to us what it *really* is that we're fighting for. For some of us, our WHY will stay the same throughout our journey and for others it will be constantly shifting, changing and growing as we too change and grow. Our WHY doesn't have to be complex. It might be as simple as having the freedom to love wholeheartedly, the ability to spend more time with your family, or the means to travel the world.

How our WHY Helps us Face our Fear

In order to find our own WHY, we really have to turn the focus inward. *Why* do we want to pursue this dream? What will it *do* for our lives and the lives of those we love? What will be *gained* in the end?

Let's walk through a simple exercise to help pinpoint our own WHY. First, think about what you really want. Are you building a business and dream of being wildly successful? Do you live alone and desire to find love? Are you unhappy in your career and want to do something different? Do you struggle with what you see in the mirror and really want to lose some weight and feel confident? Knowing what we want is just the first step in working to achieve our goal. The second and far more important step is understanding *why* we really want it.

To truly envision our own WHY, we need to ask ourselves why we want to pursue this dream in the first place and then dig deep to answer that very question - "Why?" - over and over again until we find ourselves thinking, "Yes! That's it! I'm willing to work for this!"

In order to help us envision the process, let's walk through a couple of scenarios together, starting with the example of a single working mom who is toying with the idea of starting her own business.

She asks herself: "Why do I want to build this business?"

"I need more money, because we're so tight all the time."

"Why?"

"Because I'm tired of worrying at the end of each month, wondering if we're going to be able to pay all the bills. I'd like to have freedom to do more with my kids and create more memories, to have some extra wiggle room."

"Why?"

"I can already see my kids worrying about our struggles with money. They're getting older, and they need to enjoy being kids and not worry about living paycheck to paycheck."

"Why?"

"Because not having enough is scary. I need my children to feel secure. I want to help them out when they're older. *I need* to feel secure. I need to know that I'm not going to be a burden to them down the line."

Security. That's her why. Security is what will drive her to work on her business when one of her ideas fails. Security is what will cause her to get back up after bawling her eyes out because she was afraid it was all going to fall apart. Knowing that her financial future is secure and her children are taken care of is her big WHY. Her eyes are opened and she knows her dreams are possible. Her dreams are bigger than her fears, her WHY will pull her through, and she will not give up.

Let's take a second example of a top-level executive who longs to quit her job and open her own coffee shop.

She asks herself: "Why do I really want to do this?"

"Because I hate my job. I hate getting up each morning and pretending that what I do makes me happy. I'm miserable. I haven't been truly happy in such a long time."

"Why?"

"Because my job has me so stressed out – meeting deadlines I really don't care about, assessing goals that have no meaning to me, missing out on important family milestones. I hate the person I've become, and I'm not really enjoying life anymore, just *surviving* it."

"Why?"

"Because I can only imagine what it will feel like to finally live life on my own terms and build my own dreams instead of spending so much time building someone else's dream and trading a huge portion of my own life in order to do it. And even though I went to school for years and have worked so hard to get to this place in my career, what I really want to do is be happy, and to help others do the same. And I'm just not happy."

"Why?"

"Because I love coffee and opening a coffee shop has been something I've talked about for years. It will bring me joy to be able to brighten people's days with a good cup of joe. It will make me happy to provide people with a warm and inviting space to meet and laugh and maybe even escape from the same stress I'm feeling right now."

Freedom. That's her WHY. She wants freedom from the daily grind and from building someone else's dream. She has discovered what she's passionate about and what will fulfill her. She knows the changes she needs to make in order get there. Her insatiable desire for freedom will get her through all the criticism she'll face when people question her decision to give up her career. Her dream of freedom will get her through the fear of turning in her resignation letter and taking that leap into the unknown. She can see clearly for the first time in a long time, and she knows that her WHY will get her through.

In this next story we see how Tracey's focus on her WHY has pushed her out of her safety net and allowed her to boldly - although not without fear - walk into her destiny.

∞

TO LIVE FEARLESSLY MEANS TO DEFINE THINGS FOR YOURSELF AND TO KNOW YOUR PURPOSE. WHAT I'M DOING RIGHT NOW FORCES ME TO NOT BE AFRAID TO MOVE INTO THE POSSIBILITIES BECAUSE I KNOW I'M DOING WHAT I WAS CALLED TO DO IN LIFE. I CAN'T STAY IN THE DARKNESS.

- TRACEY

Tracey is a 46-year-old wife, mother, coach and visionary who helps women face their fears of transforming and transitioning into a place of happiness and wholeness and living their life's purpose.

When I think of fear, the first word that comes to mind is uncertainty. Right now I'm experiencing a major transition in my professional life, with leaving the safety net of my career to build my own life coaching business. And my transition into entrepreneurship has been scary.

Before starting my new coaching business, I had taken a pretty straightforward professional path - from high school to college and then into my career as a paralegal and later as a teacher. I've always done a wonderful job of doing the "right" thing, and yet I knew that my life was calling me to do something different.

My coaching centers around helping other women face their fears of transforming and transitioning into a place of happiness and wholeness and living their life purpose. I'm a very confident person and that's one of my greatest strengths as an entrepreneur, but it also causes me to be afraid that I may not reach the women who I want to reach, or that they may not believe I'm providing them with enough value. I've been doing a lot of mindset work around this fear because my philosophy is "I know we have everything inside of us." I believe this, but I've had to work hard to pull this belief out of myself.

So many of the women I work with are in denial about their own lives. Society tells us that there's a ceiling on what we can do, so I think we often *stay* stuck just to fulfill what we think is expected of us, knowing that it's not what we want deep down inside.

I was leading a vision board party the other day with a group of really successful women - doctors, attorneys, engineers, lawyers. They were on a path that most people would describe as very successful, but many of them, when we really got down to it, didn't know who they were or what they really wanted. I took them through this exercise where they had to write down what they envisioned for their life. And many of them couldn't do it. So I then asked them to just write down three things they enjoy doing in life. And many of them couldn't even do that. They just didn't know. And this makes me sad.

In some cases, I do think fear can be a good thing. In my life right now it's pushing me to do what I need to do because I value my message and believe that my work is important. My big dream is to have conferences, purpose retreats and workshops that bless women all over the world. I want women to know that they don't have to remain stuck and I want them to create a vision for their lives.

It's so freeing when you're living in your purpose, when nothing else matters except for what you're doing and not too much can ruffle your feathers because you know that as long as you're able to do *this*, then everything is fine. I want every woman to have something to get up for in the morning, and many people don't know what it's like to get up in the morning and be ready to enjoy what you're doing.

My work now forces me to not be afraid to move into the possibilities, because I know I'm doing what I was called to do in life. I can't stay in the darkness. To live fearlessly means to define things for yourself, to know your purpose, and to just move through your fear. If this book has any message about fearlessness, I would hope that it would be to face your fears and push through them. Because you don't want to deny any part of yourself. You want to face your fears, get to the root of them, and then move forward in your purpose.

∞

The lesson we learn from Tracey's story is that our WHY can help us move forward and act in spite of our fears and, as she describes it, it's the *lack* of a strong WHY that often keeps women stuck in the same place year after year, afraid to try new things and follow their dreams.

Getting Personal With Your Big WHY

Now, stop and take a minute to think about your big dream. Whether it's finding security in building your own business or finding freedom through opening a coffee shop, changing the world through service to others or opening your heart up and letting down those walls – close your eyes and ask yourself, "Why do I want this?"

Once we have our first answer, we need to ask the question again – "Why?" We need to keep drilling down until we get to the heart of why this dream is so incredibly important. And we have to remember that sometimes the WHY that pushes and propels us forward is not always found in the future, but might also be rooted in our past fears or what we're going through right now, in this very moment.

In essence, our WHY might not begin with looking at what the future holds, but with simply finding freedom from our past in order to move forward with the ability to live freely and wholeheartedly. So let's keep drilling down. We'll know we've arrived when we get there.

The moment when we clearly see our WHY might be so powerful that it brings us to our knees. It can be both freeing *and* scary at the same time. It's like putting on a new pair of glasses and suddenly our vision is sharp. We can see so clearly that we long to reach out and grab what's in front of us, steal the happy ending, and run across the finish line – but we can't. It's just not within our reach. Yet.

However, it can and will drive us through those moments of failure and defeat, and those times when we're so tired that we just want to give up. In the end, our WHY will push us toward our happy ending and that goal we so strongly desire to achieve.

So write down your WHY and put it somewhere where you will see it every single day. Every time you see this why, you will be reminded *why* you're taking those steps toward the very fears that used to paralyze you.

Once you have owned your WHY, pursuing it may not be comfortable. You will have to actively work through each deep-rooted fear that has created your fear boundary, call it out for what it is, and overcome it. But as long as your WHY is strong enough, it will make everything you're going through worth it. Your WHY will drive you each time you want to escape back into the known, the safe, the comfortable. Your WHY will pull you through.

So then why have we tried to move forward so many times and then just ended up quitting as soon as we've experienced failure? Why have we simply given up, even when we've known our WHY and know in our hearts and souls that we really do want to push for this dream? Why have we not continued pushing when the times were tough?

We've quit pushing because we have allowed our fears to be bigger than our WHY. We've allowed our fears to speak to us from within and tell us, "You can't do this. You'll fail. You're not worthy." And so we give up and allow these voices to fuel our excuses and to stop us from pursuing the dream that just a moment before we had told ourselves was the most important thing.

We can silence our fears and grab onto our WHY as we continue to move forward by taking a deeper look within. In fact, it's the next step that we have to take in order to start letting go of the fear and learning to live fearlessly.

Kerri shares this lesson with us in the following story, as we see how her ability to move past her fears and leap into the unknown created opportunities that she couldn't have even dreamed of earlier in life. Along the way, it was her WHY and her willingness to remain teachable that led her to fulfill some amazing goals.

∞

IT'S ABSOLUTELY NOT EASY TO BE A WINNER. I'VE ALWAYS TOLD MY DAUGHTER THAT, TOO. YOU CAN GIVE UP AND MAKE IT EASY AND THAT'S OKAY, OR YOU CAN GET GOING, WORK REALLY HARD AND GET TO THE OTHER SIDE OF YOUR FEARS.

- KERRI

Kerri is a 48-year-old beauty and wellness coach, salon owner and educator with a 30-year career in the beauty industry. She has owned her own salon for 10 years and has been a network marketing professional for five.

I felt fear when I left my family's beauty school business and cut ties for a few years because my relationship with my parents had turned so toxic. Leaving that comfort zone and venturing out on my own was scary because I had worked for and with my parents for a long time. I was also leaving the safety net of a steady salary, and even though the environment had grown unhealthy, it still felt safe.

One morning shortly after my 40th birthday, I just woke up and decided I couldn't do it anymore. I had had an altercation with my stepdad and decided that it was the very last time I was going to allow him to verbally or emotionally abuse me, as he had been verbally abusive to my mom and me for years. It was hard to deal with the abuse personally and it was hard to watch my mom – who was the powerhouse behind the business – always take a backseat to his ego.

I remember walking out the door of the beauty school that day and just knowing that I was done. I left with no idea of how I was going to pay my bills or anything. I did have my own salon, but it was barely making enough at the time to pay for itself.

I slipped into depression in the period following this. I drank a lot and really tried to bury all my fear and the feelings that came with it. Looking back, I think I was just so afraid of leaving the shelter of my family business and wondering what I was going to do with my life. My car got repossessed, I received a drunk driving citation, and I could have lost my house. I think going through all of this was like God tapping me on my head saying "Ok, if you keep doing what you're doing, then nothing is going to change."

I had to start asking people for help. This was hard for me, like I think it is for many women, because we fear that if we ask people for help then we are weak. But this is so far from the truth. I believe that God puts people in your life at the right time. Certain people have come into my life who have been like, "Let me show you this, let me show you that. Let me show you about marketing, let me show you how to run a business." I think I was coachable and open-minded enough to say, "Ok, show me. I'll go to that meeting with you or I'll read that book or I'll go to that seminar."

I had some small moments along the way when I acted like a spoiled brat, getting angry that things weren't falling into place. But I never truly wanted to throw in the towel once I started my business, because I had made a commitment of five years. So after three years, my salon was breaking even and making a little bit of money. Now I'm 10 years into my business, financially free, and still going strong.

Getting to this point was not easy and I just had to keep powering through the hard times. It took lots of sacrifice, investment, time, energy and tears to get to the place I am today. I know that if I let up on the gas pedal I could end up right back where I was. So I have to keep moving forward and keep the momentum going.

Joining a network marketing business has been the most life-changing thing. It's why I can say at 48 years old that I really don't have many fears. I do a lot of personal development and am surrounded by so many people who are positive and doing great things. I used to care about what people thought in a way that I just don't anymore. I've been through so much now that if I worried about the opinions of others I would be in a ball huddled in the corner most of the time.

When you emerge from something difficult you realize how strong you really are. You know that you screw up and you fail daily and that as long as you're failing, you're learning - if you take the time to absorb the lessons. I always look back at how far I've come, then I look forward and go, "Oh my gosh, look how much room I have to grow!"

That's why I've done so much personal development. Before, I was broken and I had to fix it. No one else was going to come and save me. I had to start empowering myself by reading, going to meetings and seminars, and being around positive and successful people. I knew that if I didn't fix myself then I was going to be leaving a messed-up legacy for my children and grandchildren. I want to leave a different kind of legacy - an earth-shaking, wow, she-was-here-and-look-at-what-she-did legacy.

Knowing younger people are watching you gets you out of your comfort zone. Your life's a movie, and you get to decide whether they're going to repeat your story in a good or bad way. So that motivates me. I want my story to inspire others in a positive way.

I think it's amazing what a person can accomplish if she just stops feeling sorry for herself, gets down, works hard, digs in deep, and stays focused on what she needs to do.

It's absolutely not easy to be a winner. I've always told my daughter that, too. You can give up and make it easy and that's okay, or you can get going, work really hard and get to the other side of your fears.

∞

Our WHY can compel us to move forward regardless of our past and our fears, as it did with Kerri. For some of us, our WHY is already so clear in our hearts and minds as we read this, and for others of us, we might know that we're getting close, but that we still have some searching to do. Wherever we might be on our WHY journey, it's important to understand that our ability to overcome our fear, pursue our dreams, and get unstuck during those times when we feel paralyzed is all connected to the WHY that motivates us.

CHAPTER
7

THE SUPERHERO NEMESIS TO THE FEAR VILLAIN: THE SECRET POWER OF A POSITIVE MINDSET

∞

We all make mistakes, have struggles,
and even regret things in our past. But you
are not your mistakes. You are not your struggles,
and you are here NOW with the power to shape
your day and your future.

– Steve Maraboli

Once we know our WHY, we have the compass that will help us to navigate this often difficult process of really letting go of our fear. And this, my friend, is where the hard work begins. It's where we start to build a stronger self-belief and actively work toward creating a more positive view of both ourselves and the world. And it all begins by learning to take control of our thoughts and interior conversations, because only then can we develop the positive mindset that we're going to need to overcome our fears.

Imagine you walk outside on a beautiful summer morning. The sun is shining, a light breeze is blowing, and there's a smile in your heart. You know it's going to be a *great day*! You walk over to your car, hop in, roll down the windows, and start humming along to a song on the radio as you begin your drive to work. As soon as the next song comes on, you're suddenly drawn into the memory of the last conversation you had with a friend. It wasn't a good conversation, and you start to get a little upset and think, "Why did she say that? Who does she think she is? Doesn't she know that she's not perfect either?"

The conversation continues in your head, as you let her know exactly what you think and give her a good piece of your mind. Without even realizing it, your grip tightens around the steering wheel, your teeth begin to clench, and that good feeling you had earlier is gone. By the time you get to work, you're not only irritated, but you carry your bad mood into the office and before you know it, your entire morning has been ruined. You're overreacting to coworkers, every email that comes into your inbox seems overwhelming, and you just can't seem to shake the general feeling of irritability that you know has nothing at all to do with anything in your office.

We can go so quickly from being in a wonderful mood, ready to conquer the day, to becoming upset or angry. One memory can easily trigger some deep emotion from a past hurt, injustice or fear. And that emotion can steal our peace and put us into a place of unrest, anger or perhaps even self-hatred.

The biggest danger of holding these interior conversations, where it's just us against our imaginations, is that they can be very undermining and get past our defenses undetected. Many times we don't even know that we're having these conversations until we catch ourselves smack dab in the middle of one. In fact, there's so much going on inside our heads that it's fairly easy to get caught up in these thoughts and allow them to hold us captive without even realizing it. Think about it – have you ever been driving for awhile on a long road trip and then suddenly realize that you don't even remember driving for the last half hour because you were buried so deeply in thought?

Even though there are so many things that can catalyze these internal dialogues, most of the time the reason our minds are so quick to jump into one of these battles is to protect our hearts and justify the things we did or did not say, the things we regret doing or not doing, and the times we were hurt or taken advantage of. The emotions that are a direct result of entertaining these thoughts can easily steal our peace as we get into the habit of defending ourselves or standing up for others in our own imaginary space.

Why We Fight Battles in Our Own Minds

So why do we allow ourselves to get angry, to be upset, and to sometimes even get physically sick over a conversation that isn't even real? More often than not, the root of these exchanges where we judge others and put ourselves down is fear, and we're simply scared.

Remember how we said that fear is a lack of safety and a fullness of the unknown? Usually when we're in the middle of an interior battle of epic proportions, we're feeling vulnerable and unsafe. Perhaps our interior conversation is rooted in the fear of being unlovable or unwanted. Perhaps it's the fear of failure. Regardless of what the root fear is, it often hits us like a cannon blasting right through the wall, the fear boundary, that we built to protect our hearts. We quickly try to close the gap and seal it tight by putting up all of our defenses and shooting the enemy down as fast as we can. Sometimes this manifests in the way we talk to ourselves when faced with our root fears.

When we get caught up in these interior conversations, whether we're talking to ourselves or others, the root is often the same – fear. And once we recognize this, we can stop holding so tightly to the stories we repeatedly tell ourselves. We can stop pretending we have it all together. And we can stop blaming everyone and everything for the way that we feel and the anger we hold on to.

Changing the Tracks

It's pretty amazing how intricately we were designed and how much we have yet to learn about the power of our own minds. We can control our mind and use it to our benefit to help us grow and become stronger, or we can allow it to take over like an out-of-control, behind the scenes super-villain, running our lives and taking us down a destructive path.

In order to stop this vicious cycle from stealing our peace, we *have* to change the tracks – the interior conversations we have with ourselves – that continually reinforce the very fears we're trying to leave behind. We need to know that allowing our minds to run rampant can be very destructive to both ourselves and others around us, as our thoughts turn to action and keep us from conquering our fears and living out our dreams.

If we can get into the habit of catching and stopping our interior conversations right when they begin, we can then immediately redirect our thoughts elsewhere. In learning to change our mindset so quickly, we can save ourselves a ton of heartache, anger and frustration.

So how do we learn to change the tracks that have been playing for years? How do we silence the voices that have been whispering fear into our hearts, telling us, "You're unworthy. You're unlovable. You're a failure. You're completely and utterly worthless?" How do we stop that kind of negativity from seeping into our hearts and ruining any chance we might have of truly conquering our fears and learning to love ourselves?

The first step we need to take in changing the tapes is to *stop* the dialogue. As soon as we realize that we're engaged in a self-destructive interior conversation, we need to immediately decide that we will no longer participate in that conversation.

This is so key! We have to *desire* change enough to stop the conversations before they completely take over. In the beginning, there will be many conversations to interrupt. We have to be on guard, because it's extremely easy to get caught up in giving someone a piece of our mind that it takes every bit of our willpower to stop the argument. But that's just it – we're *giving* them a piece of our mind, a piece of our sense of well-being. If we want to change our attitudes and ultimately our lives, then we *must* change our mentality, stop these conversations right when they start, and not allow our minds to go wildly unbridled.

Next, we need to have a go-to thought or mantra ready to help us make a quick switch. The key here is to redirect our thoughts before we have time to really mull it over. For example, you may have a go-to thought or mantra such as "I can choose peace rather than this" or "Give me grace." Or you might have an image or person that you can think of in order to help draw you out of that conversation. It doesn't have to be anything epic; it just has to help us train ourselves to quickly take that leap out of the depths of our interior world within seconds.

The third step is to decide where our mind will go from here. When we find that our emotions are taking over and we're too wrapped up in our own heads to see things clearly, we can completely switch gears and step back from it all for a minute before moving forward.

Imagine we're in a room, a fight breaks out, and we're so upset that we're ready to start throwing punches. We can either stay there, get into a knock-down, drag-out fight and walk away bruised, or we can quickly exit the room, take a few minutes to calm down and then figure out how to deal with it once we can again think clearly.

We can start to do this by immediately switching to our go-to thought and then quickly moving our mind to something more substantial. For instance, we can think about the next project at work or home or start making a mental list of everything we have to do this week. Or we can do something as simple as putting on our favorite song and having a good jam session. The point is to *do* something that will take us away from the emotion of the interior conversation that we were just entertaining, and transition to a less emotionally charged train of thought.

Choosing Compassion

As we grow and train ourselves to step back and take a clear look at the bigger picture without getting dragged back into those all-consuming thoughts, we can then begin to see through yet another set of eyes – eyes that remove pride and judgment from the table – and start to look through eyes filled with compassion.

With practice and time, we can catch ourselves in the depths of conversation and instead of holding on to judgment and anger, we can jump to our switch mantra and then transition to a more compassionate and productive train of thought. When we realize that we honestly don't know what is going on in the mind and heart of the "antagonist" in the story and when we understand our own deep-seated fears and *why* we become so defensive, we can begin to have compassion toward ourselves and others. This helps us let go of these fearfully charged emotions and decreases our destructive interior conversations over time.

With practice, we can become pretty good at taking control of these thoughts, skipping the go-to thought and getting right down to business. Now, whenever I catch myself in a heated interior conversation with a friend, family member, or someone who's hurt me in the past, I immediately stop the conversation and switch to prayer. My prayer usually goes something like this: "Lord, please bless this person and help her find healing." That's it. It's not always easy to say this prayer for someone who's hurt me, but when I do it puts my heart at rest so that I can peacefully move on to something else.

Learning to Set Boundaries

It's important to distinguish between compassion in our interior conversations and setting boundaries in real life. There are usually reasons people act the way they do and we can work to be compassionate toward them. However, if someone is hurting us emotionally and/or physically, then it's time to set a boundary and perhaps even remove this person from our life.

While we should be compassionate and understanding, we also need to know that we deserve to be respected. Therefore, we must set boundaries even when it might be difficult to do so. In fact, in many cases we may need help from a counselor, psychologist or good friend to help us take the leap. We also need to realize that it's *okay* to ask for help. In the end, by setting boundaries, we come to realize that yes, we are *worth* being respected and are worth more than what we maybe have been accepting as "normal" in our lives.

When we *don't* set these boundaries, it's often because we're afraid. We're afraid of what people will think. We're afraid of being rejected or of being unlovable. And sometimes, we're actually afraid of being physically harmed.

When we allow people to cross necessary boundaries, we freely hand over the keys to our hearts to someone who is unworthy of holding them. And only the worthy should be trusted. Take Thor and his mighty hammer or King Arthur and the sword. Only the worthy could lift the hammer or pull the sword out of the stone. When it comes to our hearts and our vulnerability, only the worthy should have access to the keys that unlock them. When someone is tearing us down instead of building us up, when someone is either emotionally or physically hurting us, then it's up to *us* to set a firm boundary with this person, protecting ourselves, our hearts, and sometimes even our bodies and our lives.

Just like with most everything else, the root cause of us not speaking up against those who hurt us, *not* removing toxic people from our lives, not setting our boundaries often shows up as – you guessed it – fear. As we've said before, this fear is so powerful that we're often willing to sacrifice our well-being, and sometimes even our physical and emotional safety, because we're afraid of what someone else is going to think or do. And even if these fears are real – for example, we might fear physical retaliation from someone who has caused us harm in the past – we need to not let them paralyze us. We have to bring our fears into the light, call them out for what they are, and value ourselves enough to work through them. It may be the hardest thing we've had to do in our lives, but we have to know *we're worth it*.

How many times do we allow others to cross lines that should never be crossed? How many times do we rationalize their actions and come up with excuses for them? In all honesty, it's probably too many times. We were created to be respected, so we not only deserve respect from others, but also need to be able to stand up for ourselves if we're not receiving this respect and say "enough." Many of us want to be rescued from our struggle, whether it be by a friend, family member, or knight on a white horse, but the reality is the only person who we *know* can rescue us is ourselves.

When we are able to clearly set boundaries, we're saying to ourselves, "I'm worth more than this." And the more we practice this skill, the easier it is to know when it's time to say "enough" and when we need to work at letting go and moving forward.

Remaining Teachable

Having a positive mindset is one of the most important steps we can take toward not only living out our own dreams, but also setting an example for future generations. In order to change our mindsets, we have to cast out those negative voices. We have to let those fears know that they will not control us. We have to stop the interior conversations and then fill that void with something positive. We have to *learn* how to love ourselves. We have to *learn* to see the ways that we are valuable and can provide value. And we have to learn how to set boundaries.

After we take back control of our mind and stop the conversations, we can replace those negative tracks with a new stream of positive ones. We can read and listen to books that help us understand *where* we need to make the changes and give us the tools we need to actually follow through. We can seek out mentorship from those who are further along the path than we are. We can take stock of all the negative influences in our lives and replace them with more positive ones.

It's important to continue to develop a positive mindset if we want to grow, face our fears, and overcome them. Whether we call it continuing education, meditation, daily devotionals, or something else, when it comes to personal development we need to find what works best for us and make the decision to become intentional and consistent with it if we really want to experience the change we seek.

Our minds are amazingly powerful tools that many of us don't even know how to harness. It's like having a wild stallion on your ranch – beautiful from afar, but also dangerous because of its unbridled and uncontrollable strength. Now take that same horse, bring in a horse whisperer, and with some effort, training and love, that same wild horse is still powerful and beautiful, but also bridled and well-trained, and goes on to win many races. Our minds are no different – it's possible to train our minds and control our thoughts without letting go of our beauty or power or belief in God.

The following story is a lesson in how we can change our mindset in order to overcome our fear. Megan's fear that was directly connected to a childhood experience kept her from learning to ride a motorcycle for so long. That is, until she took some intentional steps to change her mindset.

∞

I OVERCAME MY FEAR THROUGH SELF-MOTIVATION AND MINDSET. I JUST HAD TO TELL MYSELF THAT IT WASN'T AS BAD AS I THOUGHT.

- MEGAN

Megan is a 35-year-old mother and Harley-Davidson mechanic who has learned to embrace her uniqueness and works hard to teach her children to do the same.

I'm not your usual woman. I mean, I'm a Harley-Davidson mechanic. I faced real fear when I first learned to ride a motorcycle. I was terrified of the idea because of how dangerous everybody said it was and it took a few months to overcome my fear – that gut feeling of just being petrified every time I turned my leg over a bike.

I know that this fear was directly connected to something that happened when I was a little kid because in 1984, my father was in a bad motorcycle wreck. I have a very vivid memory of his wrecked bike being pulled onto a tow truck. So I know that's where my fear came from, but it's also what fueled my drive to really want to learn how to ride.

I overcame my fear through self motivation and mindset. I just had to tell myself that it wasn't as bad as I thought. As dangerous as riding a motorcycle may be, I knew I just had to turn my fear over to God and know that whatever will be, will be. That being said, I didn't just get up one day and decide I was going to ride - I actually read books and studied the topic, because I knew that if I educated myself and gave myself the tools I needed, then I wouldn't be so afraid.

If I could share any message about fear, it would be to face your fears, no matter what they are. You just have to learn to accept fear and face it head on. If I had never faced my fear of riding motorcycles, then I never would have gone on some of the most beautiful rides of my life. It's unbelievable, the places I've seen and all the memories filled with laughter.

∞

As Megan's story illustrates, overcoming fear is often a choice that we have the power to make. Will we look at our situation and *choose* to be positive? Will we tap into something motivational to help us get over the hump? Or will we look at the struggle and the hardship and follow an easier path by simply giving up and giving in?

Making the Choice to Change

It's easy to slip into a mindset where we tell ourselves that fear is just what happens to us, that we have to accept it, and that we don't have much power to really do anything about it. But the reality is that even when we can't change our circumstances, and even if we can't stop ourselves from feeling fear in the first place, we *can* choose how we react in these situations and how we react to the fears that go right along with them. We *can* make the choice to change and to face our fears head on. With the proper tools, we can step outside a difficult situation, take a good look at the challenge we're facing, and say, "Okay! How can I tackle this? What's the best way to handle it? I'm ready!"

In our next story, Katie's response to her son's autism diagnosis shows us how powerful a positive mindset can be when facing challenges and overcoming the fears connected to these challenges.

∞

KNOWING THAT HE'S THE SAME KID BUT NOW WE JUST KNOW A LITTLE MORE ABOUT HIM HAS MADE IT EASIER. THIS REALLY HELPS TO TAKE FEAR AS IT RELATES TO HIS AUTISM OUT OF THE PICTURE.

- KATIE

Katie is a 33-year-old stay-at-home mother who volunteers at her children's schools and serves on a number of boards and committees in the community. She loves to read, hike and spend time outside.

My middle son Zachary is autistic. His diagnosis came about kind of slowly. My dad had actually suggested it, and my first thought was No way! because I had seen autistic people depicted in movies – swaying back and forth, spinning in circles – and this was not my son. Zachary is shy, but also very loving and affectionate and has always been this way with our family.

So when we learned more about autism, and it dawned on me that my son might actually be autistic, it really wasn't a shock. It was an adjustment though, and in the beginning I didn't know what to do or how to do it. I suddenly felt like I was going to have to go to battle for him all the time. I thought it was going to be me and Zac against the world.

When Zac started preschool, it was scary. Putting my three-year-old on a school bus was terrifying. I didn't know if he could handle it, but I never let him see my fear, even though it was hard for me. I had to change my way of thinking because

I needed him to be able to thrive. I'd never done any of this before, but neither had he. I knew I was going to need to make the decisions, and he was going to have to get on that school bus. I think I was like, "I guess we're going to try and do it." We did and it all worked out okay.

I'm sorry – I'm choked up now. I think our family is doing so well because of how I view my son and how Zachary is. Even though I had some initial fears before and immediately after his diagnosis because of all the unknowns, I had to reaffirm that my son was still my son. He's easygoing, and our family is not restricted by his diagnosis in anyway. We're pretty much able to do the things we would normally do as a family, we just now have someone who doesn't speak very much, who has an IEP, and who has help at school.

When I was first pregnant, I remember my friend telling me that being a mom was the scariest, most difficult thing a person can go through, but also that it was the most wonderful, amazing, rewarding job we will ever have. Being a mom means you have to constantly fight back fear – from checking them as infants to see that they are breathing, to stepping back while they play at the playground, to putting them on the school bus for the first time.

We don't often realize that we are constantly stepping back from fear in those little moments when we're letting them learn and grow, and possibly fail or get hurt. It's the big moments when we realize the fear is there. But we are strong because we have to be. And the kids are strong too. It is scary figuring it all out, but we are all figuring it out. Every day. We are not crazy – we are so consumed, so overflowing with love for our kids, that we forget sometimes that other moms have been there and are going through it with us. It helps to talk about it and to know that we are not alone. It does take a village! Thankfully we have a pretty awesome village here.

When all is said and done it isn't like Zac has a diagnosis that changes him. He was born this way. Once I put it like that, I was able to see that he is how he is, and this is how our family is. Knowing that he's the same kid, but now we just know a little bit more about him, has made it easier, and this really helps to take fear out of the picture.

∞

The lesson we learn from Katie's story is that we have the choice to let our challenges consume us or to develop a positive mindset and face them head on with positivity and grace. It's easy to stare at the mountain ahead of us and react with the fear and the "I can't do its" that beat us down and stop us from climbing. But if we want to overcome a challenge, then climb we must. So we turn "I can't do it" into "I *will* do it" and bravely begin the climb. We make it to the top by taking the necessary steps to learn more about what it is we're facing, to find out how others who went before us tackled similar challenges, and then to see how we can apply these lessons to our own lives.

Overcoming the Time Excuse

When we have so many things on our plates, whether they are business deadlines, extra-curricular activities for our kids, or volunteering at a local shelter, it's easy to make the excuse that we just don't have enough time to invest in personal development. When we're already doing so much, it can be difficult to even think about taking time out to read something we might just not *feel* like reading. When it comes down to it, though, we all have the same 24 hours in a day, and it's what we do with these hours that will decide if we climb the mountain or choose to stay stuck.

Changing our thoughts through personal development isn't the only way to achieve our dreams, but *until* we change our thoughts, nothing else in our life is likely to change in any real or permanent way, especially when it comes to fear. Speaking from my own experience, it wasn't until I made the decision to listen to my first personal development audiobook that I finally began to grow and to change the negative tracks that had constantly played in my head.

When it comes to personal development, how long we spend reading isn't as important as consistency. Ten minutes every day is better than an hour every once in awhile. We can take a few minutes to read first thing in the morning or before we go to bed at night or we can listen to an audiobook when we're driving in the car, washing the dishes, or running errands.

The same goes for spending time in prayer, meditation, journaling, or any other daily practice we believe is important. We can create a habit by carving out time and space at a specific time every day to pray, or we can meditate in our "day cracks" between errands or meetings or while switching laundry at home. Any free time can used as a moment to build a more positive mindset.

The key here lies in consistency. Just like with exercise, if we want to see changes in our bodies, we have to work out regularly. The same goes for developing our minds. If we want to see positive changes, then we have to make time to grow. Changing our thoughts *is* doing something, and it can often be some of the hardest work we undertake on our journey to living a more fearless life.

Staying Positive in Spite of the Odds

In the next story, we'll hear from Elise how she was able to keep her mindset positive and remain full of grace in the face of cancer. Her story is a powerful lesson in how we can make the choice to face scary situations with a positive mindset.

∞

THROUGHOUT ALL OF THIS, I'VE SOMEHOW KNOWN THAT EVERYTHING WAS GOING TO BE OKAY. I HAD THIS FEELING IN MY GUT IN THE MOMENT WHEN I FOUND THE LUMP, IN THE MOMENT WHEN MY FIRST DOCTOR CHECKED ME, IN THE MOMENT OF MY MAMMOGRAM, IN THE MOMENT WHEN MY SECOND DOCTOR SHUT HIS COMPUTER DOWN AND CRIED, AND IN THE MOMENT WHEN I LOOKED AT MY HUSBAND AND SAID, "I'M GOING TO BE OKAY. EVERYTHING IS GOING TO BE ALRIGHT."

- ELISE

Elise is a 37-year-old mother and blogger who was diagnosed with breast cancer when her youngest child was only seven months old. She is very involved in local theatre productions and loves to work on creative projects with her family. She is also very involved with You Night, a non-profit organization that benefits cancer survivors.

I have five kids and at the time of my cancer diagnosis my oldest was nine and my youngest was only seven months. I was nursing my daughter one day when I felt a lump. I thought it was no big deal at first, but at the same time I also had this sinking feeling in my gut that I knew just what it was. As odd as it sounds, since I was a little girl I always thought that I was going to get breast cancer since my maternal grandmother had it and I had heard that it skipped a generation.

So when I felt the lump, something in me said, "This is it." But at the same time, I'm a laid back person who never wants to cause a disturbance, so I didn't want to go to the doctor overzealous and freaked out. I wanted to make sure that I had checked everything out and knew what I was talking about before I even entered that doctor's office. So I asked some friends who had cancer about their doctors and treatment plans without ever letting them know that I thought I might have it myself.

Once I found out that they don't do mammograms on women who are nursing, I weaned my daughter. So when I finally did go in for my appointment, I was pretty prepared. I even had a little piece of paper in my back pocket filled with information from my research in case they told me I had breast cancer and asked me who I wanted to be referred to for treatment. As soon as the doctor checked me, he said right away, "I don't even want you to go home. I want you to go straight over to this other doctor and don't stop. I don't want to alarm you, but don't stop. I'm going to call in a favor." I pulled the piece of paper out of my back pocket telling them exactly who I wanted to see. When I looked at my husband, his eyes were huge! He had no idea that I was actually kind of prepared for this. I just held his hand and said, "I'm going to be okay. Everything is going to be alright."

Everything moved pretty quickly from there. The very next day, I was in New Orleans at one of the best cancer hospitals in the country sitting in an office looking at this renowned surgical oncologist. As soon as the new doctor saw my mammogram results, he turned off his computer, closed my folder, and teared up. He told me that in all his many years of practicing medicine he felt like I had one of the worst cancer cases he'd seen on such a young woman and mother.

The moment of my diagnosis was very eerie – I felt almost strange for feeling so calm because I'm a mom and I know I have all these kids. I felt like I should have been freaking out, but I just wasn't. Whenever I read the Bible, I like to simply open it up to a random page, put my finger on a verse, and read. I call it "Bible roulette." So I went home that night, opened my Bible, and Philippians Ch 4:6-7 was on the page in front of me. I read the words "Cast your cares upon the Lord and he will give you peace and grace beyond understanding." That verse really resonates with me. I feel like God's just given me this peace and grace that is totally and completely unexplainable. It makes no sense – *it's beyond understanding.*

Because of the advanced stage of my cancer, this second doctor referred me to another oncologist with an equally excellent reputation since I wasn't ready for surgery and needed a good six rounds of chemo first. My next doc was this cooky and wonderfully intelligent man who dressed like a pirate for fun on a daily basis. He was absolutely fantastic, handpicked by God for me and for my family.

Throughout all of this, I've somehow always known that everything was going to be okay. I had this feeling in my gut in the moment when I found the lump, in the moment when my first doctor checked me, in the moment of my mammogram, in the moment when my second doctor shut his computer down and cried, and in the moment when I looked at my husband and said, "I'm going to be okay. Everything is going to be alright."

When I couldn't sleep well during chemo, Bob Marley's song "Three Little Birds" was in my head on constant repeat and I'd just start singing the line, "Every little thing is gonna be alright." That little phrase really got me through a lot. Every time I've become nervous, every time I've been scared, or every time my kids have been afraid, we'd go back to that song line and just feel like God would shower down a supernatural grace upon us. The song was a reminder of the same "peace beyond understanding" from Philippians.

So from the day of my diagnosis, I haven't really been scared of the cancer itself, although I still do have fear. I fear that if I die, someone is going to come and take over my job as a mom and either do it better than me or do it wrong. I've had to process the fact that cancer isn't going to take away me being "Mommy." I've had to wrap my brain around the fact that being Mommy isn't about my hair, because my kids have still loved me and still thought I was beautiful even when I had patchy little spots of hair, when I had no hair, when my hair was growing back, and when I wore crazy rainbow wigs. My baby recognized me every single morning, no matter what was on my head when I lifted her from her crib. I walked in and she knew it was me right away. So I learned that cancer is not going to take away Mommy just because I might be sick and sleeping on the couch when they come home from school. That's not what my motherhood is about.

I had my whole family over one day – my brothers and my parents, who are divorced but still came together – and I just told them that we all had to work together whether we liked it or not. I told them that we all had to look forward and not back, and take one step at a time. I felt God prompting me to say, "I'm asking you to come together, to listen to what I'm asking, for us to work as one family unit. This is what we need to do if we're going make it as a team. And we're going to take baby steps. If we're going to *live* in the present then we're really going to live in the present. We have some of the best doctors in the world, and we're going to trust them because we're not doctors. We won't be naïve, yet I feel wholeheartedly that we can put our trust in them and do everything the best that we know how to do it. We're going to eat healthy, continue to make healthy choices, and take it all one step at a time. That's all we can do. That, and pray. A lot!"

I know that I'm stubborn, so every single day I have to remind myself that overcoming fear is a daily decision. Now I've done my six rounds of chemo and I've had my mastectomy and my first reconstruction surgery. I've also had radiation and am continuing one of the chemo drugs for the rest of the year.

I remember right after my diagnosis just talking to God and saying, "Hey God, how are you doing? I'm sorry for not being so afraid. I'm sorry if I've been naïve, but for some reason I'm not scared because I'm assuming that you've got this. I know that you've got this because you have to. I'm emotional and disorganized, and I don't know what I'm doing." I wrote down each one of my kids names on a piece of paper, along with my husband's name and my own name, and put it in a little urn for prayer offerings there in the chapel where I prayed and simply said, "Now, I'm just giving it all to you, God."

So, I do have fear whenever I lose my footing and lose trust, not believing that there's anything there to catch me. Fear sets in when I forget that the buck doesn't stop with me, but with the Big Guy upstairs who thankfully has it much more together than I do. As I always remind my kids, friends, family and blog readers, God's got this. I never thought I would have breast cancer, but I think it's kind of given me purpose. If I can help even just one person with my story, then that's the miracle I've been praying for.

∞

Elise chose to fight the fear and just trust. This is what not only helped her face cancer with grace, but also what helped her lead her family through the journey with positivity and hope. In the end, it's largely our mindset that determines whether we live in fear or whether we choose to fight it. No matter how hard it may be sometimes, we can make a decision moment by moment, day by day, and challenge by challenge, to actively work on letting go of our fear and keeping our mindset positive.

CHAPTER

STAR LIGHT, STAR BRIGHT, WE'RE CASTING OUT THE FEAR TONIGHT: FINDING FREEDOM IN LEARNING HOW TO FORGIVE

*Forgiveness is not an occasional act,
it is a constant attitude.*

– Martin Luther King, Jr.

At this point in our journey, we've found our WHY and learned how to take control of our interior conversations. But there's still another big step we have to take in order to conquer these deep-seated fears and finally enter into the light and find freedom. When we look at our past and connect with those root fears that have been keeping us stuck, we have to be able to let go of the anger and bitterness that are attached to our hurt in order to make room for the growth that will allow us to move on to greater things.

When we open our hearts and are then hurt, the pain often cuts so deep that we are compelled to defend and protect our beautiful hearts from ever being hurt again. So we build this fortress to shield ourselves – a fear boundary where each brick is created out of another justification for our anger or hurt, another defense to protect our broken selves. We build it strong and we build it thick to protect us from our own fears and to stop the pain – or even the possibility of pain – from entering. The wall grows as we take each instance of fear and hurt, form it into a brick, and then seal it tightly to close off yet another vulnerability. But we have to stop and ask ourselves what happens when we build walls so high and so thick that we can't even see what lies on the other side.

Imagine that we're in the middle of a meadow, surrounded by our fear boundary. In creating this boundary, we left a small opening so we can look out at the colorful wildflowers and take in the beautiful scenery. One day we're enjoying the view from our small window when someone throws a rock right through the opening and it hits us smack in the face. As fast as we can gather some bricks and mud, we seal up the window. We're protected now. We can't get hurt, but we also can no longer see the beauty that lies beyond the wall and our life now lacks vision. We're so busy guarding our hearts as a direct result of our fears that we end up not only blocking out any possibility of danger, but also inhibiting ourselves from enjoying life.

We tell ourselves that this wall will protect us from getting hurt, but unfortunately it's often the exact opposite that occurs. This wall buries that hurt so deep within that each brick added further seals in the pain and can often stop us from feeling much of anything, and certainly won't allow us to live freely and fearlessly.

Breaking Down the Walls

So how do we break free of this wall we've created? How do we end this cycle and help ourselves to let go of the fear and start dreaming? One word says it all, my friend – forgiveness.

Yes, forgiveness. When we've been hurt or wronged, it's *easy* to start justifying our destructive actions. We are created with this need and desire to be defended, so when we feel vulnerable we're quick to feel that we *need* to protect ourselves at all costs from being hurt even more than we already have been. So why would we forgive? Wouldn't that be making ourselves even more vulnerable and susceptible to being hurt?

You see, my friend, we have this tendency to view vulnerability as something to be avoided at all costs because of our innate desire to feel safe and protected. The very definition of vulnerability is "being susceptible to physical or emotional attack or harm," and who in their right mind would want *that*? Yes, vulnerability means we are opening ourselves up to a point where we *can* be harmed, but that's only half of the story. When we build walls so high that we protect ourselves from any possible vulnerabilities, we are not only protected, but living in our own self-made prison.

There's a beauty that lies within the relationship between vulnerability, forgiveness and fear. Vulnerability can be viewed as a negative force that traps us in our own self-made prison or as a positive catalyst to a whole new world of possibilities. Likewise, forgiveness can be either an impossible barrier or a necessary part of our journey toward letting go of the fear and becoming fearless. Can you see it now? In order to let go of the fear we must forgive, and in order to forgive we must become vulnerable.

The Gift of Forgiveness

When it comes to forgiveness, we have more control than we think we do. We don't need the person who has wronged us to say or do anything or to change in any way. Just as we have the control to hold on to our fears or let them go, we also hold the power to forgive. Forgiveness, by definition, means that "we stop feeling angry or resentful for an offense, flaw or mistake." The key word here is "we." *We* stop feeling angry. By definition forgiveness is not about something the other person does. It's all about us. So forgiveness is an action, an intentional choice that we have the power to make at any given moment in our lives.

The reason that we so often *don't* forgive is because we feel that in forgiving, we're telling the person who hurt us that what he or she did was okay or that we're somehow condoning what happened. We feel that in forgiving, we're giving up a piece of ourselves and our dignity. But the truth is this – forgiveness is a gift, and it's perhaps the hardest gift that we can ever give. If it's truly a gift, then the question becomes who are we really giving this gift to – The person who hurt us? The person who left us feeling unlovable or unworthy? The person who humiliated us?

No. Absolutely not. Forgiveness is the hardest and most beautiful gift that we can give to ourselves. Every time we say "I forgive you," we're letting go of the pain, tearing down those walls brick by brick, and watching our fear boundary crumble.

These walls we've built connect us so intimately with those who have hurt us the most. They bind us to the pain, the hurt, the anger, the heartache. But when we take these small moments where we're faced with a memory that immediately strikes us in the depths of our souls, and instead of getting angry we take a deep breath and say, "I forgive you," the wall we built out of the depth of our pain begins to crumble.

The Forgiveness Cycle

You see, forgiveness is intimately connected with the interior conversations we talked about in the previous chapter. When we choose to immediately stop the conversation, face our root fears, and tell ourselves that we are worth *more* than holding on to anger and resentment, we can then get to a place where we simply say, "I forgive you." In that moment, we begin to experience true freedom. We give ourselves the gift of telling our fears that they no longer control us. A gift of being able to shout from the rooftop, "You have no control over me anymore. I take back my dignity. I take back my freedom. I choose to love again, I choose to let myself be loved again, and I choose to allow myself to dream."

All this being said, it would be nice if we could simply say "I forgive you" and have it be a one time, done deal – no more hard feelings, no more struggling with interior conversations, and no more hurting. But unfortunately, although we can choose to forgive, it's not so easy to forget. Because of this, forgiveness isn't a one time, done deal. It needs to remain a repeated action – something we do moment by moment, day by day, over and over again.

I'll never forget the conversation I had one afternoon with my little sister, Beth. She was going through a difficult time and struggling with a lot of heartache and had every reason to be angry and bitter, but she wasn't. I didn't quite get how she could be so compassionate when I knew she had been so badly wronged.

That afternoon, I learned the secret behind the peace that she had found when she told me, "Michelle, I finally understand what Jesus meant when he said that we are to forgive 70 x 7 times. He didn't mean that we are to forgive that many times and that's it. He meant that we are to forgive *each instance* of a hurt or wrongdoing 70 x 7 times." And suddenly it all started to become clear *why* she was able to be at peace in the midst of a storm and how making that constant choice to forgive had made all the difference.

Over time, the pain lessens and it does get easier to forgive. It just takes practice, a lot of "I forgive yous," and a lot of letting go. It takes a *lot* of changing the conversations in our heads and loving ourselves enough to do so. It's hard work, but this hard work brings us freedom. It allows us to become vulnerable again, to break down those walls and to once again open our hearts as we begin to let go of the fears that have held us captive for so long.

Taking the Forgiveness Leap

So how do we even get started when we might still feel so hurt, angry and stuck in our pain that we can't even say the name of the person who hurt us, let alone forgive him or her? Let's start by pulling out a piece of paper and pen and writing down the names of the people we need to forgive. As we write down each name, let's not only think of the people who have hurt us, but also allow ourselves to feel the deep ways we have been hurt and how this hurt has consequently affected our lives.

The wounds that come to mind as we write are closely connected to all of our root fears that have been standing in the way of our dreams for far too long now. In writing down the names of those who hurt us, we're not only naming the hurt but also beginning to release the hold that these root fears - our fears of rejection, of being unlovable, of being unwanted or unworthy, of failing, you name it - have had on our lives.

Our second step is to forgive. This step will most likely hurt, but just as it hurts to take a splinter out of our finger or to clean a wound, it will feel better when it's over and we begin to heal. So let's look at the names we just wrote down. Look at each one and allow yourself to know and feel in your mind, body and heart exactly what you're forgiving. Then, one at a time say: {NAME}, I forgive you.

It's *so* important that we actually say the names of the people who have hurt us out loud. Every time we say their names along with "I forgive you," we can imagine our fear boundary slowly crumbling around us and our hearts opening just a little bit more as we begin to overcome our fears.

Our third step is to acknowledge that there is one more very important person who we absolutely have to forgive. Because we know ourselves most intimately, it's probably pretty safe to say that the one we most need to forgive is ourself.

We are created with such complexity that it's not always easy to understand the roots of our hurts and fears or who and what we actually need to forgive. Sometimes, the things we need to forgive ourselves for are obvious, and sometimes they're not. There's something to be said for learning from those who have already walked down a particular path. Bettye's story is filled with several lessons on motherhood and mindset, but most importantly on how she not only forgave her son and his father, but also came to forgive herself.

∞

OVERCOMING FEAR FOR ME IS ALL ABOUT FORGIVENESS.

- BETTYE

Bettye is a 63-year-old retired hotel manager, mother, grandmother and great-grandmother. She now works as the executive assistant for an educational consultancy firm and spends as much time as possible with her family.

When my son was growing up, I feared not so much for myself, but for him being out in the world without me to protect him. When he was 11 years old we lost his father. I was so afraid for him in the time immediately following his father's death. My son was an only child and I feared that he would gravitate to other men who were into things that didn't reflect how he was raised. And as time passed, all my fears came true.

My son served over 10 years in prison for drug-related charges. When he was incarcerated, my fear was that he wouldn't change while in prison, and that it wasn't going to be enough to teach him the lesson he needed.

It is hard because as mothers we are commanded to do everything in our power to protect our children. Love is our intent. My son had everything but an airplane growing up, he went to private school, and he had a car on his 16th birthday. He always had what he needed and wanted, so there was never a reason for him to do any of the things he did.

I think that the love and fear we have for our children are always going to be there, but eventually something is going to blow up because fear and love can't share the same space. We have to love our children where they are, which sometimes means loving them from a distance. When my son first went away to prison, he would send me letters asking for money and name-brand tennis shoes. It took me a short while to figure out, but I learned that I couldn't sacrifice the roof over my own head to give him what he didn't need anyway. He had room and board. He was going to survive. What I *did* do is send him an encouraging card every single day he was there. Every day for ten years he had mail. And after a while the family did it too. He knew people back home still loved him.

I wish I had known 20 years ago the ways in which I contributed to my own health issues. Stress made me do crazy things. It made me work so many hours, it made me eat on the run, and it made me worry so much about my son. I ended up having open-heart surgery for no other reason than the stress I put on myself. I know now that stress is the biggest killer because it damages everything within you. What I learned along the road of life is not to fear much because if I can't fix or control something, I have to take it out of my mind. I think this has helped me sustain myself for the last 12 years health-wise.

Overcoming fear for me is all about forgiveness. I had to forgive my son's father for dying at a time when my son so desperately needed him. I had to forgive all the men on the streets who lured my son away from me and into a life that caused him to make some very bad choices. And I had to forgive myself. If I could rewind the clock, I would pause, take a deep breath, and just tell myself, "Bettye, this has nothing to do with you. You did everything right. He made his own choices at a time he was able to make choices, and you grieved the whole time because you didn't want him locked up with criminals until you finally realized that he was a criminal too."

When my son came home from prison for the last time, he really did prove to me that he had changed. Although I didn't view it so much as a change as I saw it as him bringing forth what I knew had been in him all along. He came home, he rebuilt his life, and now everything is beautiful. He was 29 when he was locked up for his longest sentence and he's 43 now.

When I hear the word fear, I think the first thing that comes to mind is that something bad is going to happen. When I'm feeling afraid, I just dissect the fear, look at what's happening in my life, and see how I can flip it into something positive. I don't let it overtake my life anymore.

∞

We learn from Bettye's story that it's easy to not only blame ourselves for things we've done, but also to blame ourselves for things we really shouldn't – like for being seriously hurt or abused somewhere in our past, or for being neglected, whether these neglects were big or small, emotional or physical. By definition, forgiveness means to *let go* of hurt, bitterness and anger. So even when we can come to a place where we know in our minds that *we're* not to blame for the hurt, abuse, or other pain, we still need to find a way to quit being angry within our hearts – especially if we're holding on to the idea that any part of it might have been our fault. Because it's one thing to *know* it's not our fault, and a completely different thing to let go of the anger, bitterness and hurt that we feel toward *ourselves* for being emotionally or physically violated.

It's easy to be hard on ourselves for mistakes that we *have* made, whether large or small; times we've made a fool of ourselves or hurt someone without meaning to; things we *shouldn't* have done, but *did*; things we *should* have done, but *didn't*. We often judge ourselves harshly for not being perfect. And then when we don't live up to our often unrealistic expectations, we replay our failures over and over in our minds. We speak words of hate to ourselves, when what we really need is love and compassion.

In order to break this cycle, we first need to figure out how we truly see ourselves. As we mentioned earlier, we have the best seat in the house when it comes to knowing who we are, what we've done and haven't done, and what we've been through, which often makes it harder to be compassionate. We tend to speak to ourselves much more harshly than we do to others, and it's often only when we take a minute to stop and really think about *how* we view ourselves that we know what we're up against and which fears have the deepest roots. When we look at ourselves in the mirror and think, "You're ugly. You're fat. You're weird," what we're often seeing is our fear of being unlovable, of being rejected, and of being unworthy. And we have to see the fear before we can let it go.

So let's dig into what we really think about ourselves. Find a mirror, a pen and paper, look at your reflection, and ask yourself what you see. Be honest. It's time to speak truth about how you really feel about yourself. Start writing. Let's get it out of our heads and onto the paper. It's okay if it's hard, it's okay if it's not pretty, it's okay if it hurts, and it's even okay if we cry. Going through this process is so important because we can't heal until we forgive ourselves and we can't forgive ourselves without knowing what we have to forgive in the first place.

Now put the mirror down and pretend that you're instead looking at someone else who has the same characteristics that you're so critical of in yourself, but who isn't you. Write down what you see when you look at this person. Because we're often so much kinder to others than we are to ourselves, sometimes it's easier to forgive our own imperfections when we can take a step away for a minute and see ourselves through a different pair of eyes.

It might not be easy to be compassionate and to decide that yes, in spite of our imperfections, we *are* lovable and *are worth* loving and being loved. But when we change our perspective and look at who we are, flaws and all, through a different lens, it's often easier to see ourselves as being beautiful and captivating, which helps us to become more compassionate and forgiving to the person who deserves our compassion and forgiveness the most.

The last step of breaking this cycle, letting go of the fear, and beginning to love ourselves again is quite simple. We have to forgive ourselves. Period. That's it.

Let's start by looking back at the first description we wrote about ourselves and really thinking about that person as we've described her. Think about the failures or apparent failures, think about the mental picture we drew. Let yourself feel any emotions that come up, then take a deep breath and simply say, "I forgive you."

The Forgiveness Exercise

Again, forgiveness – whether it's of self or others – is not a one-time done deal. We have to forgive over and over again. Think about when we start a new exercise program. The first workout we do often leaves us extremely sore the next day. But in order to see real change, we have to keep exercising, so we make ourselves work out again. It hurts, but we do it anyway, knowing that the pain will lesson with time. Eventually, our muscles grow stronger and we are no longer in pain, but we still have to keep up with the exercise in order to remain strong.

The same goes with forgiveness. It can hurt at first. We might say "I forgive you" and not really *feel* it. With time and practice though, we grow stronger. Our self-image changes. Our fears of being unlovable or unworthy of love or belonging begin to fade. When we forgive, we're releasing the power these fears and the people they're connected with – whether ourselves or others – have held over us. We're telling ourselves, "I *am* worth it. I *am* worthy of being respected. I *am* worthy of being loved, and if you can't see that and you don't love me for who I am, then that's okay. I am *still* lovable, I am *still* worthy, and I *still* belong."

You see, the more we believe that we are worthy, respected, loved and lovable, the more we become free to be authentically ourselves, to be vulnerable and to let ourselves be seen in the world. And the more we love ourselves, the more we're able to act in spite of our fears and the less the opinions of others matter. Even though we still have fear, it no longer has a paralyzing grip on us. It's there, but we've learned to let go of its hold and we've learned how to forgive. We're not giving fear a front row seat in our lives, and we're not letting it direct the show. So fear still exists like it always has and always will, but we are no longer *living* afraid and we are finding out what it means to live free.

Our next story clearly shows the power of forgiveness in helping us to truly begin to let go of our fear and move forward. Kelley has a broken past, but through seeking help and learning how to forgive, she has been able to embrace new freedom as a mother, wife and entrepreneur.

I NEED TO NOT BE AFRAID OF MESSING UP MY KIDS OR AFRAID OF MY MARRIAGE FAILING OR AFRAID OF WHAT OTHERS THINK OR THAT I WILL WAKE UP ONE MORNING AND EVERYONE WILL LEAVE. I SEE NOW THAT I HAVE PURPOSE AND AM SO GRATEFUL FOR THIS. WE ARE BUILDING SOMETHING NEW IN THIS FAMILY, WHICH TAKES TIME, GRACE AND LOTS OF FORGIVENESS.

- KELLEY

Kelley is a 37-year-old mom who has been married for 13 years to her best friend. Together, they are raising their children in a love-filled home that strives for freedom. She has a self-admitted addiction to books and loves to share passionately with other women in hopes of helping them find the freedom that she has now embraced in her own daily life.

I will never forget the moment when I was 4 1/2 years old and my parents shared that they were getting divorced - sitting there at my dining room table, my back facing the window with my older sister on my right and mom and dad across from us. I remember feeling it getting dark behind me and hearing the words: "Your dad is not going to be living here anymore. It's not that we don't love one another. We just are not going to be together any more."

As I write this my stomach sinks and aches. It still does not make sense.

I began to cry and said "I promise I will be better!" I immediately felt it was my fault that they were getting divorced. Because if I really mattered, my dad would stay. It *had* to be my fault. I remember hiding in one of the boxes when my Dad tried to pack up his things, thinking he wouldn't be able to lift it, and that would make him stay. Sad to say, it didn't work.

Divorce is ugly. It just is. I know every person who has been through divorce says it was what needed to happen, what they needed to do. And in some cases this is true, but it doesn't take away the fact that it's ugly and it hurts kids. I was feeling bad, insecure and sad about what was supposed to be "good" for my parents. I had to start a new life that day. I told myself at the age of 4 1/2 that I couldn't trust anyone. Why? Because my security had been rocked – and I had learned that *people will leave.*

This started an inner dialogue at a young age. I didn't believe people or trust them, not even in their kindness. I had this all-consuming fear that I was not worth it, I was not enough, because if I had been better *he* would have stayed. I never blamed my dad or mom. I'd get upset with them and then I'd feel bad that I was angry and would project the anger back onto myself instead. This translated into a life of living in this lie, with this broken lens of thinking I was not enough and that I never could be, because if *I* had been better things would have been better.

My anxiety and fear led me to rebel and try new things in order to be accepted. But even then, I still saw myself as a reject. Again, I was not enough. I struggled with addiction, eating disorders, depression, anxiety and suicidal thoughts. I was constantly speaking negatively toward myself – "You're not good enough. You're not pretty. You're not smart. You're not ever going to succeed. You're lazy. You're not artistic or creative. You won't matter."

Growing up, my mom would always affirm me, but in my head I would still think, "She's only saying that because she's my mom." It didn't matter. You could say a hundred good things to me, but it was the one bad comment that would stick.

My childhood fears spilled over into this intense fear of failing as a mom. It has in many ways prevented me from being the kind of mom I wanted to be. I was so afraid of making my children feel like I had that I managed them rather than let them in. My receptivity was the biggest part of me that was damaged that day of the divorce announcement. I didn't want to receive. I was not worth it.

Anxiety settled in so intensely that I didn't want to live because I was so broken. Every time my family struggled, I felt it was my fault. My kids' troubles with friends, their illnesses, their learning struggles, my husband's work struggles – they were all *my* fault.

There was this hardened cast around me, and I remember telling my husband that I knew the kind of mother and wife I wanted to be, but I just couldn't get there and didn't understand why. I wondered, "Why can't I just go and run and hug my kids and be silly like I've seen all my friends do?" I just wanted to do that and hated that I couldn't, which of course caused me to hate myself even more.

And with my kids, instead of seeing all the good in them, I would see their struggles. I'd become paralyzed because I couldn't help them or fix their problems. I would feel helpless and blame myself for it. I would think, for example, that if I were a better mom my daughter would never lie. Or if I were a better mom my oldest wouldn't struggle with self-esteem or be picked on at school. These were all things I couldn't control but felt responsible for anyway.

The past year I've gone through tremendous healing because I knew that I had to figure out what was wrong. I couldn't handle the anxiety anymore, so I knew I needed help. Gathering the courage to actually talk to someone and being real about what I was feeling and thinking was a huge a-ha moment. When I first started going to counseling, I thought it was my wounds with my dad that I had to heal from, but then my mom became sick and was diagnosed with Alzheimer's. It was like a slap in the face, because on top of feeling disconnected from my dad, I knew that one of the people I cherished the most was going to begin to forget who I am.

There was a point when I asked my husband, "Why didn't you leave?" because my dad left me and now I was losing my mom too. I was really scared. It helped when my husband told me he was not going anywhere. He's been a huge rock through all of this, because I know he's not leaving me. He helps see the truth in me. He doesn't think I need to change. He wants me here, and his patience and forgiveness have been essential.

I remember when I met my husband in college I tried to scare him off by spilling my story, my drama, my darkest sins, thinking he would run from me. Instead he said "That makes you even more beautiful, because I can see how God is pulling you through and has never let you go." This was not what I expected to hear. He was my first safe person, someone who wouldn't leave. And in that safe place I started to unpack the junk of my life and forgive.

I forgave my dad to his face for not being there, for not knowing how to love me the way I needed him to, and this took years. I'll never forget what he said "Please love me for the dad I am. I can't be the dad you think I need to be. I am doing the best I can." It was like I saw him as a person for the first time. I had to revisit that wound just last year and forgive him again, and this time I was able to experience gratitude for all the ways he did try, realizing he has his own wounds and baggage.

I forgave my mom for moving me away from my dad, for the mistakes she made in her life and the ways she tried and failed, and I started to give thanks for the friendship I found with her. It took *years* of spiritual direction, reading, journaling, counseling and praying to process everything, but layer by layer I forgave. And when these wounds pop back up, when the scar aches, I forgive again.

Forgiving *myself* was another story. I refused to look at myself for so long. Why? I was not worth it. I would rather focus on others – give to them and shine on them. I realized that if I didn't forgive myself, though, I couldn't love my kids. If I didn't forgive myself, I couldn't receive love from my husband. And if I didn't forgive myself, I would pass this brokenness on to my children.

I started to see that when things happen and go wrong and don't make sense, I don't have to take ownership of them. I learned to give myself grace, and by doing this myself I'm able to teach it to my kids. I started to crave their hugs, and to enjoy time with my husband rather than isolating myself. My belief that the world would be better if I was not here began to fade.

If I used to run up out of the blue and hug my kids, they'd love it but also think it was weird. But now they're getting to know me for the first time. I've been letting go of the perfectionism and letting them in more and more. And it hurts! It hurts because I see how limited I am, but at the same time that hurt heals because I am loving and being loved. I am connected and being vulnerable and healing. And I've realized that it's okay to mess up because it's more important to feel loved.

Today I embrace the chaos with more confidence, and I continue to move into a place of greater receptivity. I want more freedom. I have forgiven myself for the ways I hurt my family with my anxiety. I have forgiven myself for the bad choices I made growing up. And I have forgiven myself for believing the lie my whole life. Though this is the wound I still have to revisit and keep forgiving.

I need to not be afraid of messing up my kids or of my marriage failing or of what others think or that I will wake up one morning and everyone will leave. I see now that I have purpose and am so grateful for this. We are building something new in this family, which takes time, grace and lots of forgiveness.

∞

Kelley learned how to name her root fears, is actively working on changing her mindset, and has discovered how to forgive both herself and others. As a result, she now lives a life where she is letting go of her fear and embracing freedom. Her story teaches us what is possible if we're willing to do the work.

By making the commitment to forgive those who have wronged us, we can begin to let go of the baggage that has held us in fear and prevented us from living out some of our biggest dreams. We have to let go of the bad to make room for the good. The lesson we learn here is that when we know our WHY, change our mindset and learn how to forgive, we too can really let go of our fear and embrace the freedom that comes with living a fearless life.

WHO'S AFRAID OF THE BIG BAD WOLF: FACING THE FEARS OF CHANGE, SACRIFICE AND FAILURE

∞

Always do what you are afraid to do.

– Ralph Waldo Emerson

When we get to the point where we can clearly see our dreams and when we can name and claim the specific fears that show up along the way, then we will finally know what we are up against and what exactly we're fighting for. Whether it's fighting to become financially free, fighting to overcome a disability, or fighting to change our mindset, when we can see beyond the difficulties of our daily lives, we can *choose* to live boldly in the midst of our personal circumstances, *choose* to get back up every time we fall, and *live* in the face of our fears.

Transitioning from the place where we're simply *talking* about our dreams to where we're freely pursuing them is not as easy as it may sound, though. When we stop and think about it, how many times have we started something and then quit? We know what we want. We start to go after it. We're moving forward, and then suddenly, we're standing there unable to take the next step. We want to continue on our way, and yet we can't quite put our finger on why we're stuck.

If we're honest with ourselves, most of us are much better at talking about what we want to do than we are at actually *doing* anything. And when it comes to overcoming fear, we're really no different. Once we've named and claimed our fears, we start to move outside of our safety zone. And it's at this point that many of us are going to be stopped dead in our tracks without really understanding why. It is no longer the immediate fears of rejection or not belonging or danger that hold us back, as we've already worked through those. But there are a few other fears we encounter as we're about to take that leap from *thinking* about trying something new to taking action.

After working through our root fears, our walls are down and we should be able to freely breeze through them. We often don't, however, because in taking this all-important step we know that our daily routine will have to radically change. That we're going to have to give something up, maybe a *lot* of things, in order to make this change. And the thought of doing all of this and yet possibly still not succeeding is, well, scary. So in order to actually succeed, in order to really stick with it for the long haul, we *have* to face three new fears – fear of change, fear of sacrifice and fear of failure.

Fear of Change

Doing something different is such a simple, but often intimidating concept. But why is *doing something different* so scary? Why do so few of us actually do what we say we want to do? Why do we fear change? We fear change because when we do something different, we really have no way of knowing the absolute outcome, and fear is the lack of safety and the fullness of the unknown, right? We fear change because we know we'll be uncomfortable. We fear change because we open ourselves to potential risks and become vulnerable.

Perhaps one of the things that makes fear of change so complex is that it looks very different to different people. For some, fear of change is rooted in what we have *known* and the fears that come from our hurts, past failures and other experiences. For others, fear of change is so deeply connected to fear of the *unknown* – the many "what ifs" that we're constantly pondering. What if I fail? What if I can't pay my bills? What if I don't win? Same fears, but now projected to the future. Fear of the *inevitable* is when we know that change will bring with it a certain amount of discomfort. One of the scariest things about change is that when we *do* make a change in our lives, whether large or small, we often can't ever go back to how things were before, even if we want to. And that, in itself, is *scary*.

Change is hard no matter how we spin it, and with Stacey's story we see just how scary the decision to change can be – even if we believe in our hearts that it's what we need to do.

∾

I WANT MY DAUGHTERS TO KNOW THAT WHEN YOU DON'T KNOW WHAT THE ANSWER IS, YOU JUST HAVE TO LISTEN TO YOUR GUT AND THEN YOU WILL HAVE LESS FEAR. I WANT THEM TO NOT LET FEAR GUIDE THEIR DECISIONS, EVEN AS THEY GET OLDER AND HAVE MORE RESPONSIBILITIES.

- STACEY

Stacey is a 52-year-old mother of two daughters who has been married for over 20 years. She is a therapy director in a large urban children's hospital and is passionate about yoga, spending time in nature with her family and friends, and good food.

I've been thinking for some time about leaving my marriage and this comes with a lot of fear. I know I can take care of myself, but I'm afraid of how my daughters will react. I'm afraid of losing my relationship with them, and I don't want them to turn away from me. If leaving my marriage shifts things in my community, I don't want to lose any of my friendships. So it's a fear of change, but also of loss. I'm afraid of making a wrong decision. I'm afraid that I'm wrong for even thinking of leaving.

Recently, I've really had to distinguish between the feeling of fear and the feeling of sadness. If I'm going to change my family around by getting divorced, then that makes me really sad. There's a difference between fear and sadness, but sometimes they're just wrapped up together and it's hard to pick them apart. And now that I know this, I think if I just allow myself to feel the sadness, maybe it will go away someday.

It takes so much courage to make big decisions like this not based on fear because they're so complex. And if you're really busy like I am – with a stressful career and the responsibility of raising two daughters and keeping it all together – you sometimes don't take the time you need to be quiet and listen to your intuition. You're always running on empty, taking the next step without listening to what you're supposed to do. When it's just yourself, it's easier to act in spite of your fear. When you have things and people you're responsible for, it gets scarier.

But if you know what you're supposed to do, then you have to have the courage to follow through and act in spite of your fears. I want my daughters to know that when you don't know what the answer is, you just have to listen to your gut and then you will have less fear. I want them to not let fear guide their decisions, even as they get older and have more responsibilities. You can become so stagnant when you're afraid of things.

You know, a few months ago when I was asked about being interviewed for this book, I really started to think about fear in a way I hadn't before. And I realized that I'm walking around with all this fear I didn't even know I had. I'm so afraid of everything and I don't think I've had a good, solid core that has been guiding my decisions. And yet I know that no matter what happens in the future, it's going to be okay.

∾

Stacey's lesson shows that one reason fear of change is such a big hurdle for many of us is that even though we might be experiencing an *external* change, so much of what happens on the outside either affects or is affected by what's going on *inside* of our hearts and minds.

Internal changes are often harder to explain to others because sometimes they don't quite mirror external changes. Often, when we try to tell people that we just *feel* different, that we want more, and that we're no longer willing to settle, some of them might become uncomfortable or even threatened. Their actions get to us, and then we start second-guessing whether our desire for change is even valid: "Shouldn't I just be happy with what I have? Why am I always feeling like there's something more for my life? Everyone around me seems to be just fine with the way things are. Is it wrong for me to feel this way?"

So we find ourselves at a crossroads. We have to decide if we want to continue cultivating our desire for something different, face the unknown ahead, and make some changes in our lives, or if we want to just stay in the place where we're comfortable.

Let's say your dream is to move back to your hometown. You've been planning it for years, and now it's time to actually make the big move. Suddenly, you start questioning: "Do I really want to do this? Do I really want to move across the country just to be in my hometown? Isn't this town just fine?" You begin to have that all too familiar feeling of fear and you begin to panic. "What if my kids don't make new friends? What if I don't make new friends? What if our new job prospects don't pan out? What if we're not happy there? What if? What if? What if?"

We begin to seriously rethink making the move, because on a deeper level we're afraid of the unknowns ahead of us. Those "what ifs" again emerge, the fear grows, and before we know it we've talked ourselves down from pursuing our dream of moving back home. All because of the fear of change.

How we act in the face of our fear of change will make the difference between whether or not we move closer to our dreams. Once we recognize that the fear of change is what's keeping us stuck, we can either choose to stay stuck or to feel afraid, but act anyway. And this is where the dreamers are separated from the dream followers – those of us who dream without action and those of us who actually *go after* our dreams with intention, purpose, and an unwavering focus on a our WHY.

Fear of Sacrifice

"It must be nice to be an author. It must be nice to have abs. It must be nice to work from home. It must be nice to run your own business. It must be nice to have time to go on vacation with your family." How often do we fall into the trap of telling others "It must be nice?" when we're often just afraid of the sacrifices *we'd* have to make in order to get to where we want to be in life and to achieve what we're so quick to admire in others' lives?

Perhaps the fear of sacrifice is one of the greatest fears that keeps us from going after our dreams and actually *doing something different*. We get into a comfortable routine. We have the TV shows we like to watch, the books we like to read, the extra free time to do this or that. We don't have to worry about the stress of feeling like we might fail or be rejected. In all honesty, we really don't have to risk anything – except, of course, our dreams.

Imagine we're excited about a new venture. We've set our sights on running a marathon. Our big dream is to actually *finish* the marathon. We finally wrap our head around getting past the fear of doing something different, get excited, sign up for the race, and announce our big goal on Facebook. We can practically see ourselves crossing the finish line, satisfied and victorious.

We're *really* excited about this new challenge and even convince a friend to train with us. So we come up with a plan to build up our endurance over time, knowing that it's going to include some sacrifices like getting up earlier, eating differently, and committing a lot of time to running and cross-training. The first couple of weeks, our motivation is soaring. We stick to the plan we've carefully laid out and get up at 5 a.m. like clock-work four days a week to run, have a good healthy breakfast, and plan our day.

After the initial excitement wears off, however, we begin to miss that extra hour and a half of sleep in the morning. We start to think that maybe two or three morning runs a week might be just fine. We don't really have the time to do all this running anyway. We're tired in the morning, and at the end of the day we just want to kick back, relax and get comfortable.

It doesn't take long before we convince ourselves that our dream of running a marathon was silly to begin with. We stop setting the alarm clock, begin to replace our drive with excuses, and before we know it we've fallen right back into our same old routine. The day of the marathon comes, and no surprise, we don't actually run, but our training partner does. When she calls us after the race to tell us all about it, we manage to feign excitement, even though in our heads what we're really thinking is, "I wish I had stuck with it. I wish I hadn't made so many excuses. Why did I quit?"

But what actually comes out of our mouth, after we've congratulated her, is our own verbal justification of why she achieved something we didn't. So we tell her: "Must be nice to have all that time to train for and run a marathon! I wish I had that kind of time!"

When failure manifests itself as making excuses, comparing ourselves to others, and feeling angry when we see others achieve what we've failed to, then it's a pretty good indication that perhaps we didn't make the sacrifices needed in order to do what we said we wanted to do in the first place. So what does making sacrifices have to do with fear? Well, we fear the exhaustion that comes with getting up at five in the morning. *Loss of comfort.* We fear the sore muscles and strain on our lungs that come with pushing ourselves hard in our exercise. *Pain.* We fear not being able to drink a glass of wine to relax or not being able to get lost in our favorite TV show. *Stress.*

When following our dreams, it's not always easy to make these seemingly small but necessary sacrifices. Because we're afraid of making these sacrifices, we often insert excuses as to why we can't do what we said we wanted to do in the first place. Although in the short term, *not* sacrificing doesn't seem to make that much of a difference, in the long term, these sacrifices make the biggest difference in the world.

Over a period of time, exercising and pushing through the pain *will* lead to significant changes in our bodies. Repeatedly turning off the TV and reading a good professional development book instead *will* change our mindsets to be more positive. Exchanging that second glass of wine for a meditation or prayer session to destress and clear our heads *will* make us more compassionate and connected to those we love. And exercising instead of eating those cookies *will* move us closer to our weight loss goals.

There's no way around it. With every dream comes sacrifice. We might have to let go of something we had in order to make room for what we want, even if it's letting go of something we really enjoy or value, in order to make room for something better. When we make these sacrifices, we are in effect prioritizing our lives. We're showing, through our actions, that some things really *do* matter to us more than others at a given moment in time.

If we're starting our own business, perhaps we have to consider giving up our favorite TV shows to start reading more personal development books or working long and hard hours. If our dream is to lose weight and feel confident in our body, perhaps we'll have to give up some of our favorite foods, alcohol or weekend rituals – things that we might enjoy, but that aren't going to move us closer to our overall health and fitness goals.

It's easy to get *excited* about a dream. It's easy to *decide* to go after it. It's *not* easy to actually *achieve* it. If we look at any famous athlete, we can see that it took years of training and sacrifice to get to the point where she is at the top of her field. The same can be said for the best musicians, successful business owners and writers. It's very rare that someone walks into an opportunity and becomes successful without putting in a lot of hard work and sacrifice beforehand.

So when we decide to follow our dreams, we have a big WHY to help push us through and we really want to succeed, we have to be willing to go the distance and do what it takes to get there. We have to be willing to keep putting one foot in front of the other when we just want to lie down and quit. We have to be willing to learn from the success of others and pay attention to the *journey* they traveled and not just the outcome they achieved, and then use this knowledge as we pave our *own* road and build our *own* dream.

We have to battle the "I can't do its." We have to fight the fear that we're just not up to making these sacrifices. We have to push through the tears and frustration that show up along the way, and we have to actually make the sacrifice of not giving in to our emotions and just calling it quits.

If we truly *want* to succeed, we *have* to make sacrifices. There's simply no way around it. We can't just say that we want to be an Olympic figure skater and then take ice skating lessons once a week and think that's going to get us to our goal. No, we actually have to get up at ungodly hours in the morning when everyone else is still sleeping. We have to be willing to fail time and again and put up with the bumps and bruises we get along the way to the gold medal.

How Our Sacrifices and Goals Connect

Because not all dreams are created equal, we don't always have to give up everything in order to reach them. The amount of sacrifice our dream requires is often in direct proportion to its size. When we have *big* dreams, such as winning an Olympic medal, building a multi-million dollar business, or losing 100 pounds, we have to be willing to sacrifice and to give whatever it takes if we want a true shot at reaching them.

These sacrifices we need to make and the goals we want to achieve are so intricately connected. One of the main reasons that we often fall short in life is that we're not really honest with ourselves about what we're going to have to sacrifice to actually fulfill our dreams. It's *fun* to talk about dreams and goals and it's *exciting* to envision a life far greater than the one we're living now. It's *invigorating* to think about reaching our potential and becoming the highest versions of ourselves. This is the dream-building stuff.

But the sacrifices that we'll have to make to get there? This is the not-so-fun part of our journey, which is why we're so quick to make excuses as to why we can't do what needs to be done. It's *not so fun* to wake up before dawn when everyone in the house is still cozy in bed so that we can have an extra hour in the morning to work on building our business. It's *less than exciting* to stick to a nutrition plan so that we can achieve our weight loss goal. And it's *not so invigorating* sacrificing moments with our friends and family in order to carve out the time needed to finish writing a book.

Sometimes we need a push to get started, because the more we allow ourselves to stay comfortable, the further away our dream becomes. So we have to get up! We need to stop wishing and start doing. Sacrifices are what dreams are made of, so we have to decide to take action and just do it. We can't think about how much we have on our plate. We just have to ask ourselves, "What can I do right now that will get me closer to my dream? What sacrifices do I need to make to get to where I want to be?"

The hard part is that sometimes the things we need to sacrifice are actually good things, such as setting aside a specific business goal in order to follow the dream of writing a book or sacrificing a family vacation in order to pay off a credit card and reach the dream of financial freedom. Most of the time these sacrifices are not permanent, and in the end the sacrifices we do make often facilitate more freedom down the line. For example, we might be able to use the publication of our book to reach an important business goal, or we might be able to use our newfound financial freedom to not only go on a family vacation, but also to pay for the entire trip in cash.

Although sacrificing might not seem fun or exciting or invigorating in the moment, the results of these sacrifices are the stuff that our dreams are made of. Literally. This, my friend, is the moment when we're able to walk into the highest vision we have for our lives and separate ourselves from all those people who wish without action and dream without sacrifice. Is it going to be scary? Of course! But our fears start to fade the moment we begin to take action.

So let's take some action. What sacrifices do we fear? Why do we fear them?

When you close your eyes, start dreaming, and get that strong urge to actually do something different, what is the first thing that comes to mind when you think about what you'll have to give up? What sacrifices will you need to make on a daily, weekly, or possibly permanent basis? In order to visualize these sacrifices and in order to intentionally pursue our dreams, we have to dig deep and ask ourselves these tough questions. We have to consider - When we give these things up, what will we gain? Is it all actually worth it? It's important to think about this carefully and to see how each sacrifice will impact our ability to achieve our dream and bring us closer to our goal.

Now get a piece of paper, and write your big dream or goal down at the top. Then brainstorm all the sacrifices you'll have to make in order to achieve your dream. Name them.

Once we have our sacrifices named, let's directly connect them to our dream or goal so that we can clearly see how what we give up will be worth it. This will be especially important on those difficult days when we're struggling to stay on track and our fears start to take over.

Now let's make a second list for ourselves so we can visually draw the connection. Get out a new piece of paper and write down the following:

In giving up _____, I will gain _____.

Make the list as short or as long as you need. Your list might have five statements on it or it might have 25. Again, the size and number of sacrifices we'll have to make are usually directly connected to the size of our dream. Not all dreams require a ton of sacrifice, but many do.

Now let's take that list and put it somewhere we can see it every day – on the bathroom mirror or refrigerator or car dashboard. In fact, let's put it right next to our WHY, so when we feel like giving up we have a powerful reminder as to why we started in the first place, and we'll be inspired to make the necessary sacrifices to continue to move forward and maintain that focus on our dreams.

Fear of Failure

Fear of failure is a huge obstacle for most of us. But *why* are we so afraid to fail? When we dig deeply into the roots of our fear of failure, what we often find is that these roots connect right back to Maslow's hierarchy of needs that we discussed earlier.

For most of us, when we're going after our dream, the root of this fear is directly connected with Maslow's third level – love and belonging. If we fail at love, we fear becoming unlovable and unwanted. If we go after a dream of becoming a famous singer, musician or athlete, we work hard, and then we "fail," what do we really have to lose? Perhaps it's the respect of others. Perhaps we will suffer the "I told you so" comments or the knowing looks. But in all honesty, is the fear of failure a *real* fear in this case, or is it one of those perceived fears? Are we truly in danger, or are we in a situation that we can get through without suffering any real harm or risk to our safety?

For example, if we're getting ready to go skydiving, we'll probably feel some type of fear. We're a bit terrified to jump, but we know that a parachute is on our back, and that – more than likely – we'll land safely on the ground. The same goes for following our dreams. Most of the time, what we fear will not really cause us harm in the end, and even if we fail, we haven't put ourselves or those we love in any real danger.

It would be different if our dream were to help protect our country by joining the military during a time of war. In that case, fear of failure might very well be connected to a real and scary fear that returns us to that first level of Maslow's hierarchy. In this situation, we might suffer PTSD, dismemberment, death and possible loss of family. This would be a case where we would have to evaluate our dream, and, if it's big enough, say "I'm willing to make the sacrifice should the sacrifice be asked of me."

The same can be said on another level of dreams that involve a huge financial risk and the possible loss of some of our basic needs defined on the second level of Maslow's hierarchy, including shelter and clothing – or at least at the level of comfort and security that we're used to.

Fear of failure is perhaps the most paralyzing fear for those of us who struggle with perfectionism. We have this expectation that everything we do has to be as perfect as can be. We truly believe that failure is just not an option. In fact, we spend so much time trying to get it just right that it takes us five times longer to finish any task, if we finish at all. But hey, at least if we do get it done, it's done right, *right*? Not exactly. One of the biggest problems with perfectionism is that when things don't go the way we plan, when they start to fall apart, and when we're aware of the possibility of failure, it's as if we feel our world crumbling around us.

Learning Requires Failure

It's easy to see failure as a negative. We run a race, we don't win, and so we fail. Right? We host an event, hardly anyone shows up. We fail. Right? We start a new friendship, but it doesn't end up working out, so we fail. *Right*? Well – not exactly. In life, from the day we're born, our ability to learn and grow stronger requires us to fail. Over and over again.

We don't celebrate our first birthday and then suddenly just get up and start walking. First we have to scoot, then we have to start moving our knees as far under our belly as we can. Then we're on all fours rocking back and forth. One day, we grab on to the edge of a small table nearby and try to pull ourselves up. We fall. We might shed a few tears, but we try again and again. Before long, we're walking along furniture and tables, and then one day we get really brave and decide to attempt that first step. We take one step, and then BOOM! We fall. We get back up. We try harder this time. We keep falling, but each time we get back up and try again. Before we know it, we're walking, then running.

The same can be said for any major accomplishment. Very few people just jump into something new and succeed on the first try. We have to boldly walk through our fear boundary and take the chance that we will most likely fail. We have to move forward with determination, knowing that we can get back up, dust ourselves off, and try again. If we want to be successful, it's so important that we work through our fear of failing and rewire our brain to see failure as something positive – as just another stepping stone on the road to success. This is what Lauren does in the following story. She sees new things as a challenge and drives home the lesson that it's okay to fail as long as we can just get back up, learn from our failures, and keep moving forward.

∞

WHAT I LEARNED THROUGH IT ALL IS THAT IF YOU DON'T TAKE A CHANCE AND DON'T TRY NEW THINGS, YOU WILL STAY WHERE YOU ARE. WE HAVE TO GET OUT OF OUR COMFORT ZONE SOMETIMES AND DEAL WITH FEAR AND PAIN, BECAUSE WE LEARN NEW THINGS ABOUT OURSELVES THROUGH ADVERSITY.

- LAUREN

Lauren is a 52-year-old mother of two with her first grandson on the way. She was raised in Baltimore and spent weekends on a big family farm. She is currently happily employed as a healthcare administrator.

I remember the specific day I realized that I wasn't going to do this anymore. I woke up in a hotel room and it took me a minute to figure out where I was. I had been traveling so much and was completely exhausted and working on autopilot. When I realized I had to take a minute to figure out where I was and then another minute to realize what was going on that day, I knew something had to change. We were at a convention in Boston, and that was when I went to my boss and told her I just couldn't do it anymore. She looked at me and told me we could leave for home later that day and I said, "No. I don't mean I can't do this event. I mean I can't do this whole job anymore."

At the time, I was the director of global meetings for a corporate travel arm of a leading travel company. It was a stressful job because we needed to grow significantly in some areas and sometimes it felt like I was put into a position to really be dishonest with my customers with regards to what we could deliver.

Also, I was rarely home, and when I was I had to work until 9 at night. I was exhausted most of the time and was sacrificing my family's well being along with everything else. For the most part, my daughter wasn't raised by me as I was gone four days a week, but thankfully, my husband is a great dad and we also had strong support from his parents. In hindsight, this time renewed my respect for my husband because of all he coped with through those years. It was a lot.

As for me, I was a career person. That's what I did and everybody supported that. So when I walked out on my job, I didn't think it was a big deal. I thought I would just get another job where I could be home more. However, six months later the fear settled in as I was still unemployed and had no prospects. My fear was that we were financially on the brink of complete collapse. We had to cash in everything.

Fear came into play in a couple of ways. First there was our desperate financial situation and second when your whole identity is tied up in one thing and then all of a sudden that's gone – it's scary. I had always been a career person. I had always been the boss. All my friends made a lot of money. I made a lot of money. We were used to a certain lifestyle. We hadn't had to worry about certain things and now we had to worry about everything. Every penny.

Companies were downsizing and rightsizing and it wasn't a great job market, so while I had great references and a strong resume none of the job opportunities panned out. The fear crept in as I slowly realized that something had to happen in order to save us because it was only a matter of time until we would be in complete financial ruin.

I decided to go back to school. As soon as I made the decision, one of my good friends and business mentors ended up opening the door for me to get a job in internet marketing. The job paid less than half of what I had been making before, but I could work at home and only had to go into the office one day a week. That was a Godsend, as I was able to work and go back to school for nursing.

I never had a real fear of failure – that's not in me. The main fear I had through the whole process was my initial fear of not having any focus or money. And if we had had to file for bankruptcy or something, I felt that I just couldn't have lived with myself.

Because of what I went through, I learned that what doesn't kill you makes you stronger, and that you can live on a lot less money. My rock was – and still is – my husband. I've learned that when things start getting scary, something always comes through. Never burn a bridge. Never lose faith. Do something every day to meet your goal.

So now I've come full circle. I followed a path and did the best I could with every option. I now have my previous management career combined with my nursing adventure. That had been my goal, and now I'm living it. I am toying with the idea of getting my MBA but probably need to get my daughter through college first.

What I learned through it all is that if you don't take a chance and don't try new things, you will stay where you are. We have to get out of our comfort zone sometimes and deal with fear and pain, because we learn new things about ourselves through adversity. We need to walk slowly through these times so that we can learn from our failures. The fastest way out may not always be the best. We can always learn from our failures and do better next time. When we look at failure this way, we don't have to be so afraid.

∞

Lauren's story teaches us that freedom can come with pushing through our fear boundaries and not being afraid of failure. It's easy to look back on our own lives or others' experiences and to see how some of the most challenging times in our lives were actually the times of greatest growth. Maybe the lesson here is that if we can apply this knowledge to the fear we're feeling as we're in the *middle* of something, we can live less of our lives so afraid of what might happen when we do fail, and just see failure as part of the growth process. We don't have to wait until the challenge is over to learn the fear lesson. We can walk through and with our fears in the very moments in which we're most afraid.

When we take a closer look at what happens when we *do* fear failure, we might find that with the potential for failure comes a fear of rejection, which brings us right back to those feelings of being unlovable or unwanted. For example, we might be afraid that if we take a risk and fail we will let down our boss, husband, or parents. We might fear that they'll push us away when our failure comes to light. And as with so many fears, how we approach them today has a lot to do with our own understanding of what we've been through in the past. It's important to understand *why* our fear of failure has deeper roots so that we can learn why some of us truly fear failure while others have learned to work through it and sometimes even embrace it.

Fear of Success and Its Connection to Fear of Failure

Fear of success is one of those fears that, to many, simply doesn't make sense. Why would we be afraid of something *good*? Don't we *want* to succeed? Don't we *want* to be free to dream and actually *realize* those dreams? Don't we *want* the freedom that comes with it?

Fear of success comes into play when we begin to wonder what our lives will look like if we actually do become successful and to question whether or not we'll be up for the call. We ask ourselves, "Will I live up to the expectations of others? Will people think I'm a fraud? Will I be able to handle the work that comes with success?" As we see with Aidenn Marie's story, sometimes the fears surrounding our success are there even when we think they shouldn't be.

∞

TO LIVE FEARLESSLY IS TO BE FULL OF FAITH, TO LEAVE NO ROOM FOR FEAR. JUST BECAUSE YOU'RE AFRAID DOESN'T MEAN YOU'RE NOT FAITHFUL. BUT WHEN YOU HAVE TOTAL FAITH IN WHATEVER IT IS YOU'RE BELIEVING — THAT'S FEARLESSNESS.

- AIDENN MARIE

Aidenn Marie is a 30-year-old entrepreneur, wife and mother who recently left her job in higher education to pursue her dreams of running her own event planning and educational consulting business.

Until the point that I left my last position at the university, in every job I've ever had I've always moved up and been loved and adored. So when I found myself in a situation with my last job where I knew that I either had to leave or was going to be pushed out, it really fed my fears. I was like, "Oh my God, will I ever have faith again?"

Just this morning I had a revelation when I realized I've been carrying around this low level fear with me for awhile. I thought I was just frustrated, but then I realized that I'm really facing this fear of not being successful at something anymore.

When I first started my business I had people approach me and want to hire me to put on their events. But I told myself I wasn't ready. I thought, "What if it's so big, so huge, and I can't handle it? And what if I look bad because I took on something I couldn't handle?" It was crazy, really, because I had business that was coming to me, but I was afraid of it because what if, what if, what if.

This wasn't a new fear, though. Even before I started my business when I would get a promotion at work I'd always feel a tiny bit of fear that made me cautious. Like, "Yeah you've made it here, but you have to go ten times harder in order to keep it."

I face fear every single day now in growing my business, and I do believe that a lot of this centers around my fear of success. And yet even though I'm afraid, I know that I have to be guided by my faith. To live fearlessly is to be full of faith, to leave no room for fear. Just because you're afraid doesn't mean you're not faithful. But when you have total faith in whatever it is you're believing – that's fearlessness.

∞

Sometimes when we're afraid of success like Aidenn Marie we self-sabotage – we mask our fear as a million little things that we should have done, but didn't do, so that if by chance we fall short of whatever we really want to achieve, we have something or someone other than ourselves to blame. Other times we jump to the excuse of not having enough time or the right skill set or whatever other bullshit story we tell ourselves and others, when really – at our core – we're so deeply afraid of success that we don't even allow ourselves to get there.

Fear of success can be manifested in big ways, such as subconsciously sabotaging ourselves from being selected for the next big promotion, or in smaller ways in our everyday lives. This is what we'll see in the next story from Alison, whose fear of success stems from the pressure to maintain an achievement.

∞

I FEAR SUCCESS BECAUSE THEN I MUST MAINTAIN IT.

- ALISON

Alison is a 42-year-old stay-at-home mom who has been married for 17 years and holds a degree in communication studies.

I think we fear success because after we reach a goal there's a pressure to maintain what we've achieved. Think about it. It's hard to maintain success, because once others see our success the pressure is on. We may wonder why we'd put ourselves through the trial. If we lose a bunch of weight, people may scrutinize our movements and ask, "Should you really be eating that?"

Many people are not so joyful about our success, but when it comes to our failures, there are some people just waiting to point them out. This is where I struggle so much. For example, I felt pretty good – not great, but good – last year at the pool. But now I am scared to put on a bathing suit. I fear people will look at me and wonder if I've put back on a few pounds. I have, but only a few. They may not see the weight, but they will see my discomfort as I hide behind my towel. Why? I fear success because then I must maintain it.

I know that I shouldn't have this fear. I mean, my body has changed over the years and has softened and pooched out a bit, but I know these are the battle scars of childbearing and birth. The lines, lumps and rolls all tell a story – a story of life and the precious blessing of children. So as I prepare for summer this year and strive to be healthy, I hope to live without fear and embrace my body, a temple that housed several children.

∞

Alison clearly names her fear of success and is actively working to overcome this fear as she prepares for yet another summer at the pool with her kids. Naming our fear of failure or success is important because once we do, we can then determine whether our fear is a real warning sign of danger ahead or a byproduct of something that we've gone through in the past that actually has very little to do with the current situation we're facing.

Let's do an exercise called "What's the worst that can happen?" Let's take something that we're afraid of failing or succeeding at, and then ask ourselves, "What's the worst that can happen?" In asking this question, we can visualize all possible scenarios, analyze our connected fears, and decide whether or not they're worth pushing through.

For example, let's say that we want to start our own business.

What's the worst that can happen? We might not get any clients. People we love might not support our vision. Our business might fail and leave us unable to pay our mortgage and keep our home. In asking this question, we're really asking, "Is this a perceived fear or is this a valid warning sign telling me that it would be best to not take that step forward?"

Once we have all the worst-case scenarios laid out, *then* we can ask ourselves if our dreams are worth the risk. We can ask ourselves "What's the *best* that can happen?" We may learn how to start our own business and cultivate new friendships in the process. We might make enough money to take our family on a special vacation. We may demonstrate to our children what it looks like to act in spite of our fears. And maybe, just maybe, we might become wildly successful, change a lot of lives, become financially free, and create a legacy for our family.

As long as our best-case scenarios seem worth the change, sacrifice, and yes – potential failure – then we know we're probably on the right track.

So let's get out a piece of paper and write our dream at the top. Then make two columns – one for the worst-case scenarios and one for the best-case ones. Let's write it all out, look at the words on the page in front of us, take a deep breath, and pay attention to how we feel.

Just like when we make a pros and cons list, often the process of simply *making* the list is enough to let us know what our next important step, or even leap, needs to be. We can see the potential risks, and decide whether or not those risks are worth taking. As with all things closest to our hearts, most of us will find ourselves at the end of this journey realizing that the answers we've been seeking have been right in front of us all along.

One of the challenges with fear of success is that often those who struggle with it the most have lives that appear from the outside as very together. When I was chatting with my friend Sarah and she started sharing about how much she fears success, I was blown away because I never would have guessed that she had this deep fear. At 34 years old, Sarah is a teacher, college professor and published author who many probably think has it all together. But when we get a look into her perspective on how her own fear of success affects so much in her life, we can again see that so often fear only becomes visible when we know what we're looking for.

∞

I'M LEARNING HOW TO CELEBRATE MYSELF, TO NOT APOLOGIZE FOR THE THINGS THAT I DO WELL. AND I'M LEARNING HOW TO GET OUT OF MY OWN WAY AND NOT LET THE FEAR CONTROL ME.

- SARAH

Sarah is a 34-year-old teacher, college professor and author. She loves to run, bake vegan treats, and spend time with her nieces and nephews.

My biggest fear is definitely fear of success. I guess I'm afraid whenever I achieve something that I won't be able to handle the weight of the responsibility that comes with the success. I'm afraid that I'll get to a place where I've worked so hard to be and everything will just crumble around me. I'm afraid that I won't be able to keep up with the pace of what that success demands. I'm afraid that I won't be able to keep it together. I'm afraid that when I succeed in this area, everything else that I care about will fall apart - because I can't have it all, can I?

I'm afraid that once I get what I want I'll realize that it wasn't even what I *really* wanted to begin with. I'm afraid that others will look up to me in a way that I don't really deserve anyway.

I've always been taught that with great privilege and success comes great responsibility, and on my worst of days I think that I'm not up for the task.

I'll never forget the day that I not only got accepted to my dream college, but also received a substantial academic scholarship. I was playing in a water polo game when my mom ran up to me during halftime to show me the acceptance letter. She was *so* excited, and all I could feel was fear. What if the admissions committee realized they had made a mistake and took it all away?

Fast forward a few months to my senior scholarship awards program, when I sat there and was called up on stage over and over again - amassing more scholarship money for college than any of my classmates. I remember my dad was so happy and proud of me, but I was just afraid. I knew that I should be celebrating, but instead I was wracked with a fear that at the time I couldn't even understand.

A few years later, I found out I was going to graduate Cum Laude from college. I didn't want to talk about it. I didn't want people to congratulate me. I was proud of the hard work I had put in to get to that point and I was really grateful for everything, but I was also afraid that I wouldn't be able to live up to those two little words on my diploma.

You'd think that, especially when it came to school, things would have gotten easier as I grew older and that I'd somehow get used to the success that comes with achievement. But I haven't yet. When I graduated with my master's degree and won a big research award and had the privilege of presenting my research in front of a large audience, I couldn't celebrate it. And then when I graduated with my doctorate degree, I remember being downright grumpy in the days leading up to graduation. Afterwards, I didn't even want people to call me "Dr." It made me uncomfortable. It's taken me a lot of years to realize this, but I think it all goes back to my fear of success and the responsibility that comes with it.

I'm learning how to celebrate myself, to not apologize for the things that I do well. Just recently, I was publically acknowledged for a big achievement and for the first time in maybe forever, I was able to appreciate the moment and maybe even be a little proud of myself. It's like the fear I've felt for so long was replaced with something else - not necessarily fearlessness, but definitely gratitude. So I guess I'm learning how to get out of my own way and not let the fear control me. And to me, this feels like freedom.

∞

Whether it is our fear of change, sacrifice, failure, success or all four, if we have a big dream we've been wanting to pursue, we have no choice but to push through these fears if we want to achieve it. The lesson we learn from Sarah is that no matter how visible or deeply rooted our fears may be, and no matter how long they've gripped us, it is possible to learn how to overcome them.

We are reminded, as with so many of the stories throughout this book, that our fear often has little to do with what others see from the outside and everything to do with our own interior worlds and how we process our own experiences. We are also reminded of the need to be compassionate to the women in our lives. Even when it might seem as though they have it all together, they might also be battling a lot of fear that we don't even realize is there unless we take the time to listen a little more deeply to their stories and pay attention to the role fear plays in their lives.

10

BORN TO RUN: ACTING IN SPITE OF FEAR AND LIVING FEARLESSLY

∞

You gain strength, courage and confidence by every experience in which you really stop to look fear in the face. You must do the thing which you think you cannot do.

– Eleanor Roosevelt

It's one thing to recognize our fears – to name them and claim them. But it's an entirely different scenario when we talk about having the courage and ability to act in spite of our fears, to have the *freedom* to take that big leap toward the pursuit of our dreams. By definition, freedom is "the power or right to act, speak or think as one wants without hindrance or restraint." So when we are full of fear, it's almost impossible to be free because fear *is* the hindrance or restraint. That's what's keeping us from taking those next steps toward living our dreams and living fearlessly.

Let's look at this definition of freedom a little closer – it's a *power* or *right*. We know that through constantly improving our mindset and through our ability to forgive ourselves and others, *we* are giving *ourselves* our power back. We are giving ourselves the *right* to live free. And to do so without *hindrance* or *restraint* simply means that we're no longer being confined by the fear that has held us back. It's still there, but we're not hindered or restrained by it any longer. We know that fear is never going to go away - but we also know that we can learn to act in spite of this fear and, in so doing, we can find the freedom that we have been seeking all along.

And yet, in light of this and in light of all the stories we've shared throughout this book, it still might be easy to look at some of our own fears and think they're ridiculous. But we need to remember that if we *feel* them, then we need to accept that they *are* valid. We have to *honor* them. If we are terrified to cross the road - even if there are no cars around - because we know that someone we love was killed while crossing the road, then the fear that we feel is valid. But that's where we can now assess the fear to see if it's a real fear or a perceived one. We can ask ourselves, "Am I going to be hit if I cross this road without a car in sight? Probably not. So cross the road I must, if I want to get to the other side. There's no other way to get there."

The same goes for our dreams. If we have a dream deep within our heart and we're battling all these fears inside that have been telling us for as long as we can remember that we can't do it, that we're not worthy, that it's impossible, then it's up to *us* to stop listening to all our bullshit excuses and put these fears in their place. It's up to us to stop blaming others for what we've been too afraid to do. And it's up to us to stop waiting for someone to save us. No one else will - or should - do it for us. We have to stand up, get the heck out of our own way, and get it done.

If we want to *truly* be fearless, if that is what we desire, then we have to muster up the courage to cross the road. We have to embrace the fear we have and we have to give our dreams, no matter the size, the respect they deserve. We have to hold onto our WHY, call fear out for what it is, grab it by the hand, look both ways, and then walk.

Putting It All Into Perspective

Although we may *know* we need to start moving, sometimes we might need a bit of perspective to help us gain the courage to realize that yes, we *can* move forward and start acting on our dreams. Just looking at someone who's faced cancer or a physical hardship and has risen and pushed herself to greater things is often a great wake up call for those of us who are *not* sick or injured or facing death. Rebecca's story is the first of three stories in this final chapter of women who have been through the fire, and are choosing to act in spite of some very real fears they have faced and continue to face every day.

∾

MY CANCER CHANGED THE WAY I THINK ABOUT EVERYTHING NOW. IF I'M GOING TO DO SOMETHING, I'M LIKE, "LET'S DO IT NOW." I DON'T WANT TO MESS AROUND.

- REBECCA

Rebecca is a 47-year-old chemistry professor and researcher. She was diagnosed with and underwent treatment for an aggressive form of breast cancer this past year and spends most weekends rock climbing in Joshua Tree National Park with her husband.

Sometimes I get a little relieved to talk about my cancer, because I find that people are often weird about not even wanting to mention it. It still seems so surreal that I even had cancer because I take care of myself. I'm uber healthy.

It all happened so fast. I was diagnosed on June 30th and had surgery on the 7th of July. They said the cancer was aggressive, so I didn't really have time to think about it or process what was happening. Now that I'm through chemo, I can process it a bit - like "Oh shit. Yeah. Cancer. People die from this stuff."

Leading up to my diagnosis, I was maybe a little afraid of what was going on with my body, but denial was bigger than fear. I felt the lump in April, but I had just had a mammogram and it was clear as a whistle. So when I felt the lump I told myself it was just a lymph node or something. I was in denial all of May, because I was finishing up teaching the college semester and was like, "I don't want to have cancer during the school year." And then I went on vacation right after that and thought that I'd take care of it when I got home.

I think denial is just a type of fear, like fear gets the upper hand and puts you into this place where you just can't deal with whatever it is you're facing. So I didn't actually get my second mammogram until the middle of June. And even when they said they'd like me to see the hematologist and the surgeon, I was like, "Surgeon? Why? I don't need to see the surgeon."

I don't think I really felt afraid at the beginning of my treatment. The first chemo treatment was a little scary because I didn't know what to expect. I read up on all these cancer blogs, so I had an idea of what was coming. But I also knew that I had to take my own journey just one step at a time. I would think, "Okay. Today I'm nauseous. Today I have mouth sores. Today my hair is falling out." I knew the next day I might be dealing with something else, so I just tried to live in the moment as much as possible.

I think everybody has fear, even sometimes when we think we don't. Just look at what I was living with up to my diagnosis – that was deep fear even though I can easily rationalize it away as being something else and say that I wasn't afraid. There was a part of me that knew something was up, otherwise I wouldn't have had that first mammogram.

Every once in awhile I think about what will happen if the cancer comes back. That's an unsettledness that goes right to my stomach. It's beyond terrifying. Would I go through all the treatment again? Probably, but chemo sucks. My body is still not the same.

I think about the young ladies I've connected with as a professor, the ones I've taken under my wing, and if I could boil my journey down to a single message about fear to them I would say "Step up and live." I see so many young women not doing that. When I take girls rock climbing, I tell them, "You're going to lead this climb." And they'll tell me they can't lead anything. So then I say, "No, we're not climbing unless you lead something. I can do the work for you and you can be nice and safe and live in this safety zone, or you can step up and feel the fear." I want them to step up and I want to set an example of what that looks like.

Back when I used to play the flute, I had a teacher who told me that musicians live longer because they get a clean wash of adrenaline on a daily basis, and it washes their systems. She told me to lean into that adrenaline, and that's sort of become my motto now. For the first day of school or for any new experience – *just lean into it*.

Things aren't ever as bad as we fear they're going to be. For example, you're rock climbing and you fall – your gear holds. You don't go splat. The more that happens, the more that fear manifests, the less fearful you'll become. The fear consumes you for a brief second, but then that bubble bursts. You feel the adrenaline wash through your entire system, and you're hanging there like, "Hey, I'm alive. Cool." It cleanses your system so you can move on to a better space.

Fear is in my stomach. It goes to my gut. For me, fear means the risk is real – like I'm going to lose something important. I think the worst thing about any sort of fear is that it might control what you do or don't do, so I work through my fear by verbalizing it. By speaking aloud whatever it is that I'm afraid of, the fear dissipates almost immediately.

To live in *spite* of your fear? That's courage. Lion heart right here! My cancer changed the way I think about everything now. If I'm going to do something, I'm like, "Let's do it now." I don't want to mess around. There's something that happens between being the passive observer of your own life and becoming a warrior. You have to make a transition, and there's a huge amount of energy that goes into making that transition.

Yes, a lot of us doubt ourselves. A lot of us have fear. We think we can't become that lead climber, but we can. I believe that fierceness can be powerful and that power can be attractive.

∞

Many of us face fear, and to us it's real. Whether it's our paralyzing fear of rejection or we're actually afraid for our life, like Rebecca, we can have that same heaviness in our hearts that can keep us from wanting to get out of bed in the morning and wanting to face the day. And it can be hard to pull ourselves out of that place where we just want to give up and quit trying. But that's why our WHY is so important. When our WHY is in place, we don't give up and we do keep trying. We work hard to act in spite of whatever fear it is that wants to keep us under our covers and hiding our heads under the blankets, which is what the woman featured in our next story does every day.

Carrie shares how her love for her children and the fight in her heart propel her forward and keep her getting out of bed in the morning. This intense love keeps her fighting to push her worn-out self to hold on to every moment and consistently act in the face of her own very real fears.

∞

I PUT A SMILE ON MY FACE AND DON'T LET THEM KNOW HOW BAD I'M HURTING, AND HOW BAD I WANT TO GET ON MY HANDS AND KNEES AND BEG GOD NOT TO LET ME GO. BUT I CAN'T. IT'S HAPPENING, AND I HAVE TO FACE IT. I HAVE TO LEARN TO DEAL WITH IT AND NOT POWER DOWN AND THINK I CAN'T DO THIS. I OWE IT TO THEM. I OWE IT TO MYSELF TO TRY AND BE THE BEST I CAN.

- CARRIE

Carrie is a 36-year-old single mother of seven children who is battling end-stage cancer. Carrie's sister describes her as "one of the funniest, strongest, most caring people I know. She would give her shirt off her back to someone in need and has found such purpose in motherhood."

In one day, my life changed forever. I went to the doctor with a stomachache and left two hours later with my whole life turned upside down. I went from thinking I had a UTI to finding out that I'm dying. It's unreal.

My whole concept of life has changed and I look at everything differently now, because there are so many things that are important and honestly nobody knows how short their life will be.

I see some of the things that people worry and stress about and

I'm like, "Are you kidding me right now?" I'm facing leaving my seven beautiful children without a mom. It's one of the hardest things I've had to do in my entire life, and every day it gets harder. When I go to the clerk's office and the clerk is rude, I feel like slapping her across the face and saying, "If this was your last day on Earth, wouldn't you just want to be nice and polite to somebody? You have *no* idea what somebody is going through. If you could just smile and be polite, it could change somebody's day."

My little girls are going to be one and three, and the fact that they're going to be too small to remember me just kills me. I can't even remember being younger than seven so the fact that they're not going to know me, not going to remember the little moments or the songs I used to sing or things I used to do to help them not cry - it's one of the hardest things. I want to be their mommy. I don't want *someone else* to be their mom.

I *want* them to have a wonderful mom though, when I'm gone. I think I've found someone. But, the fact that she's replacing me, and I know she's going to be their mommy is very painful. Seeing another woman bond with my kids is killing me inside, but I'm doing it for them. I want to make sure she's going to love them like I do. I know it's not the same as having the love from their own mom, but I want them to feel love from her. This is my mommy love. I want my children to feel safe and secure and she's a caring person, the second best thing to me. I've done a lot of thinking and praying and feel like I'm making the right decision. But it's so hard.

Even my boys don't understand when I try to talk about it. My younger ones are 7 and 11, and I've been trying to prepare them so they don't go into shock. I explain that Mommy is going to be in Heaven watching over them. That I'll always be there. They ask me, "Will I be able to talk to you? Will I be able to hear your voice?" It's so hard not being able to answer these questions all the way, because I *don't* know what's on the other side. I don't know what's on the way for me, but I know deep down I will be able to watch over them. It's just that fear of not being able to fully prepare them and answer all their questions. I don't want to let them down.

I have the fear of not being able to walk my girls down the aisle when they get married. The fear of living every day knowing I promised my kids I would be there for these things, and now I'm not going to be able to follow through. That's the biggest thing that gets me – not being able to get through to my kids, my little heroes, and to have promised them things and now having to explain why Mommy can't be there.

I talk about this with my older daughters. They still have hope I'm not going to die. I say I know this, but I still want them to be prepared. I guess there *could* be a miracle, but it's more likely that I'm going to die, and I need them to be prepared. But to see the hope in their eyes, like "You can beat this, Mom!" – it kills me. I'm trying to prepare them, yet trying to have hope at the same time. It's so hard to do both. It's a constant battle with myself, with my mind. Everything.

I just want them to be okay, and I try to make that happen, but it's nearly impossible because I don't think I'll ever be quite ready to say goodbye. I try to suck it up the best I can. I have to be strong for them, but I'm breaking inside. I put a smile on my face and don't let them know how badly I'm hurting, and how badly I want to get on my hands and knees and beg God not to let me go. But I can't. It's happening, and I have to face it. I have to learn to deal with it and not power down and think I can't do this. I owe it to them. I owe it to myself to try and be the best I can.

Sometimes I have to go to the bathroom so they can't hear me. I turn on the fan and cry and just let it all out before I go back out and face them again. Sometimes I'm like, "What's the next step? What do I do next?" I get so lost because I don't know where to go from here. It's so hard to put into words what I go through every day. Having that number – the days I have left – hanging over my head every time I wake up and knowing it's getting smaller and smaller. *It's so hard.*

Fear for me is knowing I gave birth to seven beautiful children who are going to need me, and I'm not going to be there for them. Fear is knowing I have to leave them behind. Before I wasn't scared of anything, but the thing I'm most scared of now is leaving my kids. I'm so scared of that. I'm a very protective mom, and the fact that I have to leave my kids is the hardest thing in the world. It would be like hearing my baby cry and knowing that no matter how much I want to, I can't go pick her up. I can't take her pain away.

Just the fact that it's causing my kids pain is another fear, because I know *I'm* making them cry. *I'm* making them miss me. *I'm* making them hurt. It's horrible knowing I'm the mom, yet *I'm* causing my children pain which I promised I would never do. I'm supposed to be the protector, the one who kisses the owies away.

I'm trying to make my kids less scared and show them their mommy is strong and that I can make it no matter what. But it's hard. I have my good days and my bad days. There are days where I'm super sick, and I don't want to get out of bed and fight, but I draw strength from my wonderful family and my sisters. There was a time when I was very sick and in the hospital for five days. I honestly thought I was leaving there in a body bag because I was so sick. I didn't think I was going to make it. It was that scary. I thought, "This is it, Carrie!" But I fought through it.

Now I just want to fight even more because that could've been it and I'm struggling to get everything done because my time is getting shorter every day. I just want to hurry up and get the most important things done because there is so much I want to leave behind for my kids. I'm never going to have enough time, and there are so many things I want to do, but I'm doing the best I can with my family's help. I want it to be perfect. There's so much I want to leave for them to know. I have to leave this legacy.

I wish I could write a book, but I don't have the time. If I had a chance to share something with other women out there, it would be this:

We need to stop worrying about the little things in life, because those little things are *nothing* when compared to what really matters. I look at life so differently now. I wish I had enough time to tell everybody, but I don't.

We need to remember what's important. *Your family* should be number one. If I could go back, I'd do so many things differently. I would have made sure my family was always number one. In the end, that's all we have.

We can't worry so much about other people's opinions. Who cares about stupid stuff like that? For me, the hardest thing is waking up and looking at my little girl's face and wondering if this might be the last time my little baby girl is going to be smiling at me. That's what matters to me, not "Oh, does my hair look perfect today? Am I five pounds too fat?" I look at everything in a different light now. It's very scary trying to wake up and live a normal life wondering, "Could this day be my last? Is this the last time I do this? Is this the last time I do that?"

We need to teach our kids life lessons – any little things that we can teach them. Teach them strength and to know what's important and what's not important. I don't want my kids to go through life worrying about what other people think. I want them to go through life having strength and faith. I don't want them to worry about the petty little things. I plan to write letters to all my kids, and leave little things behind. I just wish I had more time.

There are some days when I don't want to get out of bed, but at the same time I don't want to waste a moment. I don't know how many days I have, how many chances I'm going to get to even wake up and get out of bed.

Sometimes it doesn't seem real and feels like I'm in a dream just waiting to wake up. Then I come back to reality and realize this really is all happening. This is my life and I need to suck it up. I want to go out with a bang, so I'm trying to do the best I can when I'm really breaking inside.

I'm a little scared to know what's going to happen to me on the other side, but I'm more worried about leaving my kids than I am about what's going to happen to me. I'm more scared of them being alone.

There are still days when I cry and it feels unfair, but I try to cry on my own so my kids don't see that it bothers me so much. I'm trying to stay strong for them so they can see how strong their mom is. I want them to be able to look up to me and see that even with all this going on, I'm still their mom.

There's no way to prepare for what's to come, because I know it's going to get worse. I know I'm going to get sicker, and that scares me too. I don't want my kids to see me sick. I want them to see me, their mommy. I don't want them to see me frail and fragile. That's one of my fears. For them to see me sick and think, "Oh, Mommy needs help! And she can't get up and take

herself to the bathroom. She stopped going to the bathroom."
The fear is that they'll not see the mommy they know. That's so
scary and I know it's going to happen here soon.

I know I have to face the fear. I feel like I have no choice
because my kids are watching me, and I have to be there for
them. They're expecting to have their smiling mommy making
breakfast for them and helping them in the morning, waking
them up and making them smile too. They're expecting that.
That's my job. I wanted to be a mom and do this, and I can't give
up on them now. I have to fight everyday for them until I can't
anymore. I will fight as long as possible, and give the fight of my
life because my kids are my world. I don't know what I would do
without them. I want to spend as much time as I can with them.
I even hate sending them to school, because I want to spend
every second I can with them.

Some mornings I'll wake up a couple of hours early just so I can
watch them sleep and see how sweet they are when they're
asleep. My mom will call me and be like "What are you doing?"
"Oh, I'm just watching my kids sleep again." I enjoy every second
of it, just lying there next to them. Sometimes I'll even wake
them up and have them come sleep in my bed so I can watch
them sleep. I know it sounds stupid, and sometimes when they
ask what I'm doing I say, "I just want to watch you guys." They
laugh at me, but it's something I love to do, because they're so
sweet and so innocent.

My little one has a personality that lights up the room, and
every time I see her she says something that keeps me going. I
just want to videotape her to hear the things she has to say to
give me that extra little spirit, and I always have that thought:
"Is this the last time I'll see her little smile?" My kids always say
these things that break my heart, and all I can think is, "Is this
the last time I'll get a hug? Is this the last time I'll get a kiss?" It's
so hard, it's the hardest thing being a mom and thinking of stuff
like this. My heart aches from all the pain. It weighs me down,
but I just keep going. I know I have to.

In the beginning I cried a lot, because I thought this was
unfair. I would think, "Why does this have to happen to me?"
But now I've accepted it. I still sometimes cry and wonder why
this *is* happening. But these are my cards. This is happening.
So I know I have to be strong and show my kids how to fight

and make the best of what I can. That's what I'm trying to do now – fight.

∞

For all we know, we'll walk into the doctor's office next week, and like Carrie, find out that we're dying – one significant moment can change our entire perspective on life. What will we wish we had done? What will we wish we had time yet to do?

When it comes down to it, we just don't know if we have one more day or many years ahead of us. The truth is that none of us really knows for sure, so we can choose to live afraid to do anything, because we allow our fears to decide what we will or will not do, or we can learn to act in spite of our fears and choose to live.

Taking the Fearless Leap

The question then becomes, why would we choose to continue to live even one more single day letting our fears control us? Why would we choose to continue to live a life smaller than the one we've been called to live? Perhaps we didn't know that our deep fear of rejection was creating an almost paralyzing perfectionism in our lives that's been keeping us stuck. Or maybe before now we didn't really know how our fear of failure was holding us back from taking that big career leap we've wanted to take. Or maybe we didn't see before now how to move beyond all the fears that grew out of our complicated past.

But here's the deal – now that we do know, we owe it to ourselves to take this knowledge and do something with it. You might be afraid. I know I have been. And yet from my own personal journey I've learned that in working through our fears we can find our strength, both individually and collectively. When we talk about our fears, deconstruct them, understand where they come from and then have the courage to act in the face of them, we can find the freedom, joy and strength that represent nothing short of the most beautiful parts of our lives.

I hope that you can now see that we have so much more power and strength than we may have previously thought. Like we've seen so often throughout this book, this is not a one-time decision to let go of our fear. Just like with forgiving those who have hurt us or working on a positive mindset, acting in spite of our fear is something that we're going to have to practice again and again.

I'm going to leave you with one final story. It's about one woman and her decision to act in spite of the fear that was spoken over her. The fear that she'd never run again. That she'd never write again. That she'd never speak normally again. It's about a choice that she made – over and over – to get up, continue to fight, and act in spite of her fears. Laura teaches us the all-important lesson that when life throws something at us, we need to keep making that daily decision to get up when we fall and keep walking through our fears – one step at a time.

∞

FEAR CAN EITHER PARALYZE YOU FROM MOTION OR PROPEL YOU INTO MOTION. WE BECOME FEARLESS WHEN WE DECIDE NOT TO LISTEN TO THE CRAZY VOICES INSIDE AND OUTSIDE OUR HEADS THAT TELL US THAT WE CAN'T DO SOMETHING OR THAT WE'LL NEVER ACHIEVE OUR GOALS. BEING FEARLESS MEANS DOING IT ANYWAY BECAUSE THE REWARD IS SO MUCH GREATER THAN THE RISK.

- LAURA

Laura is 40 years old and is married to her best friend and soul mate. She believes that she was born to be the best aunt in the world to her four beautiful nieces and one handsome nephew. She says she never backs down from a challenge and lives life to the fullest every day.

My story of living fearlessly began two years ago on December 22 when I woke up a stroke survivor. I went to bed just like you, like millions of other women, thinking about how I had to get up in the morning for work and how the following evening I was leaving to meet my husband, Aaron, and family for Christmas in Colorado.

I woke up the next morning to turn off my alarm and noticed that my head was fuzzy. For a minute I thought I was just really tired, but then I realized I had no use of my right arm from the elbow down and no use of my hand. I honestly thought I had just slept on my arm funny, but alarm bells were already starting to go off. Something was really wrong. I stood up to get out of bed and realized I had no use of my leg from the knee down. That's when the alarm bells started blaring.

I stumbled to the bathroom, fear screaming in my head. I looked in the mirror and saw my face drooping on one side. I was 99 percent sure at this point that I had had a stroke, although I didn't want to believe it. I stumbled back to my bed, Googled signs of strokes, and read that I should dial 911 immediately. Instead, I called my mother. My denial was really strong at this point – like I *knew* what it was, but I had convinced myself that I must be overreacting. In hindsight, I should have called 911 right then, but I didn't.

My mother lives 90 miles away, so it took her two hours to get to me. While I waited for my mom, I emailed work to let them know I was going to be late. In my mind, I was still thinking that that evening I'd be getting on a plane to go to Colorado for Christmas. Somehow I stumbled down the hall and took a shower, although I'm not sure how I got undressed or lifted my leg to get into the shower. I think it started to hit me when I lifted my arm to wash my hair, and my hand just slid down my head. I really just started crying then.

Somehow I managed to get out of the shower and get dressed and then my mom arrived. The whole drive to the hospital I was thinking, "What if I can never use my hand again? What if I never see Aaron again? What if I never walk normally again?" I was really afraid, but I think my denial at this point was equally strong. My head was telling me that I was too young to have a stroke, but my heart was freaking out. When we walked into the ER, they looked at me and immediately said, "Stroke."

They put me into an exam room and started asking my mom all these questions. We hadn't been able to reach Aaron at this point. The IV and the doctors and nurses swarming in and out of the room were freaking me out even more. I remember them asking me to squeeze this and push that. I remember getting a CAT scan. Finally, the neurologist arrived and confirmed that not only had I had a stroke, it had been a major one. He told me that I was lucky that I was talking at all and that I had even woken up that morning.

I started crying at that point. Yes, I felt lucky to be alive, but I didn't know if I would ever have a normal life again. The doctor came back in and told me that they were going to keep me at the hospital to run some further tests, monitor me, and set me up with appointments with occupational therapists, neurologists, and speech pathologists. Finally, we got through to my husband and he was on the phone crying – just wanting to hear my voice.

They moved me to the stroke ward and I just lay there, constantly licking the side of my mouth and trying to open my hand. I felt so helpless, and I was terrified. The nurses came in every 30 minutes – telling me to open my hand, asking me my name and birthday, checking some monitors, and then telling me to rest.

At about 6 p.m. Aaron arrived and we held each other for what felt like forever. We shed a lot of tears, because when I had arrived at the hospital that morning I hadn't known if I'd ever see him again.

That night Aaron had to cut my food for me. I couldn't brush my own teeth. I couldn't use the bathroom without assistance. I could only walk three or four feet at a time, my leg dragging and my right knee hyperextending because my brain wasn't sending the message down to my muscles that they could support my weight. I was so weak.

Later that night, I felt this warm, tingling sensation in my arm like when it wakes up from being asleep. In that moment, I thought for the first time that maybe I was going to beat this. The tingling lasted only a few seconds, but it was such a strong sensation. I called the nurse over, so excited that I was getting feeling back. She told me not to be too excited about it because it was probably nothing. I could have let my fear overtake me here, but to me the tingling in my arm was a sign, and that was *everything*. I knew I could work with that.

The next morning, I called my best friend in Seattle whose wedding was two weeks away and told her everything that had happened and that I wasn't going to be able to make it to her wedding. We cried together and just hearing the fear in her voice, after seeing it in my mom and husband and feeling it myself, was awful.

I hung up the phone and tried to eat my breakfast, but couldn't stop crying. The woman who shared the room with me had the curtain around her bed, and even though I couldn't see her and never even learned her name, she spoke words into my life that day: "Young lady, you listen to me. I had a stroke years ago. Don't make the same mistakes I did. The first two weeks are critical. Don't you lay in your bed feeling sorry for yourself. You work on your recovery every day and stay positive. I sat in my bed feeling sorry for myself for two weeks and when I finally got out of bed I was so stiff that my body didn't want to listen to me. Don't make that mistake. You have a lot to live for."

I really let her words sink in. I can hear her voice even now. She was discharged shortly after our conversation, but her words forever impacted my life in a way I'll never forget.

Later that same day, a dietician came in and said, "Here's the food pyramid. Eat this and you'll be fine." Then my occupational therapist came in and gave me a piece of advice that changed my life forever. She told me, "Laura, don't listen to that dietician. Eat brain foods - pomegranates, blueberries, oatmeal, dark chocolate, avocado. Eat as much as you can and only eat organic produce. Eat protein, but don't eat dairy because it could hinder the recovery of your brain."

I was discharged at 9 p.m. on Christmas Eve. Aaron and I went home and that entire night he did not stop holding me. For a long time after my stroke I was afraid every single night to fall asleep because my stroke had happened at night and I was terrified of having another one. To this day, the first thing I do when I wake up is open and close my hand to make sure I didn't have another stroke.

We spent Christmas in Sacramento with my family. At the time my nephew was five and my niece was two, and to see how they reacted to me was hard to take. They were scared. They gave me a wide berth when I got up to use the bathroom. It broke my heart seeing them that way, and when we got back in the car to leave I just started crying.

I tried to put my hand up to keep it elevated, and I couldn't so I just sat there and cried. Aaron told me I needed to snap out of it. He reminded me that I had just been discharged from the hospital less than 12 hours ago and that I had come so far already. The whole way home he made me practice my speech. He told me to pull up a sports app on my phone and read all the teams' names. He didn't baby me in my recovery. He was like, "Nope. That's not how you say it. Say it again." It was exhausting, but it helped. I had to push forward.

When the doctors discharged me from the hospital, they had said I would be out of work for a minimum of six weeks. Less than a week after leaving the hospital, I had my first appointment with my regular physician. He ran a bunch of tests and then told me that if I worked really hard and followed all the treatment plans from all the therapists that I might get back 65% of what I had before my stroke.

I physically recoiled when he told me this. I said, "What are you talking about - 65%? I'm active." He said, "Nope. You're not going to run again and don't count on ever having full use of your hand. You may or may not speak with a lisp moving forward." Part of me was heartbroken and afraid and another part of me was like, "You don't know me. You just challenged me and I accept your challenge."

When we got home from the doctor's office that day, I started researching the brain and anti-inflammatory foods, nutrition and exercise. Aaron asked me what was going on in my head, and I told him that the doctor didn't know what he was talking about. Aaron said, "What do you mean?" And I replied, "Just watch me."

He then asked me what my recovery goals were and I told him that I had two - to write again with my right hand and to complete a half marathon in four months. I looked at him and said, "I'm going to cross that finish line either crawling or walking, but I'm going to cross it." My husband said that he fully supported my plan as long as my doctors and therapists thought it was a good idea.

So the next day I shared my goals with my occupational therapist and physical therapist. I hadn't even been cleared to walk yet, but all I could think about was those wall crawls and wall sits I had been shown how to do in the hospital. So I just did wall sits and walked along the wall every day. I had a chair next to me in case I fell and couldn't go for very long periods of time because I was still pretty weak.

Every time I felt discouraged or wanted to quit, I kept holding on to my WHY. I never wanted to be that afraid for my health again and I never wanted to see my family that afraid for my health again either. I was determined to live life to the fullest.

Ten days after my stroke I was cleared for moderate exercise, so I decided to push play on a workout DVD. Even though it was a high intensity workout, I followed along to the best of my ability. When they did a squat in the workout, I did a wall sit. When they did a lunge, I bent my knee a little bit. I modified the modifier, which was still high intensity to me. After that first workout I slept for two hours. I was physically wiped out, but I felt so accomplished. I told myself, "I'm going to do this, and it's going to get me strong."

Over and over, I visualized myself crossing that half-marathon finish line and writing. I reverse engineered those goals. I bought myself a stylus for my iPad and a cursive writing app for my phone. I pressed play on the workout DVDs every day and after only a week I was strong enough to walk the entire length of my house without assistance.

After two weeks, I was able to walk down the street. And after four weeks I could walk around my neighborhood. A walk that used to take me 15 minutes would take two hours, but I didn't care. I was ecstatic. It was again an "eff you" to the doctor who had told me what I couldn't do. My therapists were blown away at my recovery and when I told them what I was doing, they were astounded. They were like, "You're not the same person who was here two or three weeks ago." Mentally I was stronger too, because I was using my brain, eating brain foods, exercising and challenging myself.

At that point, I was walking on a treadmill. My foot would slap down with every step - walk, slap, walk, slap - but I didn't care. I kept going. I still couldn't hold my silverware. The first time I put on a bra normally I just cried tears of joy. The first time I tied my shoes, I totally lost it and cried my eyes out.

I went back to work in part because I just wanted to feel normal again. I was going stir crazy. I followed doctor's orders and only worked four hours a day, but it got me walking because I had to walk from the bottom of the train station to get to the office. Later I took the stairs and it took me a good 15 minutes to get up them. I probably could've napped for two hours after every climb, but I was like, "Nope, you need to get yourself stronger Laura."

I knew that if I wanted something different, I had to do something different. This was a new concept to me when I first heard it, but I believed it because if I wanted to achieve my goal I needed to work. I had to ask myself: "Are you willing to give up the life you had? Are you willing to give up running again? Are you willing to give up that sense of freedom again?" I knew the answer was no. So I climbed up and down those stairs everyday. I walked on that treadmill everyday.

Then I started jogging – 30 seconds the first day, a minute the second. Everyone around me would look at me when they heard that big flop of a foot on the treadmill. And when I wanted to give up, I just told myself, "Nope. You've got goals." I still did my workout DVDs too because I needed to get my legs stronger. And I still went to therapy.

The time for the half marathon came and I traveled with a friend to the race in Washington, D.C. We were running with a group in honor of her friend's daughter who had passed away from cancer at a young age. And so I told the group my story of why I was running and they were astounded. They asked me how I was even there and my reply was simple: "Because they told me in the hospital that first day that I would never run again. I had to show them I could."

I was able to run the first two miles of the half marathon. I stopped at every monument to take a picture. I didn't care what my finish time was. I was like, "There's the Capital! There's the Washington Monument! Cheers!" It took a bit of a toll on me not only physically, but emotionally as well.

I crossed the finish line and just kneeled down and bawled like a baby. I had no doubt in my mind that I was going to cross the finish line, but to actually do it was incredible. I was like, "I showed them. I showed myself."

Every stroke survivor should feel this incredible and should be able to get his or her life back. If I had listened to the doctors, if I had let the fear that I would never be back to normal take over, I wouldn't be here right now. I wouldn't have run that half marathon. So now I look every day in the eye and say, "Game on. What do you have for me now, life?" I have overcome so much that I really do feel unstoppable. There's nothing life can throw at me now that I can't handle because I know what I've overcome.

Now my biggest fear is having another stroke, and this fear propels me forward on my health journey. I know I have a second chance at life and I never want to take my health for granted again. The biggest takeaway from my stroke is that I wasn't making my health a priority in my life before. I put my friends, my family and work above my own health. Now I'm an advocate of making health and wellness a priority in life, because I learned the hard way that if you're not well, your family's not well.

I've learned that fear can either paralyze you from motion or propel you into motion. We become fearless when we decide not to listen to the crazy voices inside and outside our heads that tell us that we can't do something or that we'll never achieve our goals. Being fearless means doing it anyway because the reward is so much greater than the risk.

∞

It's women like Laura who give us a great example of what we *can* do when we name our fears, claim them and then choose to actively work to overcome them. Every day, she had to get up and push through the fear that was spoken over her by her doctor. Every day she told herself, "I *can* write. I *can* speak normally. I *can* walk. I *can* run."

Just like our very first story in this book where the doctor spoke fear over Tara's life, Laura made a conscious choice to not let the fear spoken over her life by someone else define her. And both Tara and Laura actively chose to say "Enough!" and to act in spite of their very real and valid fears.

So whether the fear we face comes from within our own hearts or from some external circumstance, whether the fear comes in the face of a real and life-threatening tragedy or an everyday need to feel that we're loved and that we belong, we *can* overcome our fear. We *can* walk through it and with it and, in so doing, we can *choose* to live a bold and fearless life.

CONCLUSION
CREATING A LEGACY
OF LIVING FEARLESSLY

∾

Live, love, laugh, leave a legacy.

– Stephen R. Covey

I hope you now see that no matter where we come from, no matter how we may have let our fears control us and wreak havoc in our lives in the past, we can start today, right in this very moment, and begin to build a different future for ourselves and a different legacy for those we love. Living fearlessly is no longer some far-fetched dream, but is a *real* possibility that's sitting right in front of us, just waiting for us to take hold and run with it.

My a-ha moment didn't come until I was 36 years old. I'll never forget the morning when I made the decision to change my life. I was tired of allowing what others thought about me – or what I *thought* they thought about me – to decide if my day was going to be good or bad. I was tired of compromising myself and my beliefs because of my paralyzing fear of rejection. I *wanted* something different, and I wanted it badly enough to do what it took to get there. I had a big WHY. So I downloaded my first personal development book and started listening and learning. I named the fears that were keeping me stuck. I began to claim the hold they had in my life. I worked hard to change the tapes and stop the conversations. I learned how to forgive again and how to push through my fears of change, sacrifice and failure.

As I became more and more passionate about living fearlessly,

I started to really think about the Bible verse Psalms 139:14, which states, "I praise you for I am fearfully and wonderfully made." I questioned at first what it meant to be *fearfully* made, so I did some research and what I found struck me right in the heart.

The fear described in this verse is the same fear articulated in verses that talk about the "fear of the Lord," which means to be *full of respect and reverence.* Emotion swept over me as I began to understand exactly what it meant to be *fearfully and wonderfully made.* I was *created to be respected.* All of the times that I had been hurt, all of the times that I had been disrespected, I hadn't felt that I was *worthy* of respect. And so it hit me – Yes! I *am* worthy of being respected and was created to be treated as such. This was so key in my own healing. So I began to set boundaries and started the work to overcome my fears and act in spite of them.

Over time I became more confident and began to see that I was *worthy* of dreaming and that I could even be successful. Not only did I become passionate about living fearlessly, but I also became passionate about helping other women find that same freedom. My friend, I'm here to tell you, that if I can do it, so can you. My prayer is that through reading this book, you have found *hope* and *vision* and have discovered your *purpose.*

So let me ask you again. Do you *dare* to dream? Will you allow yourself to take that bold and fearless leap? To break down the walls that tell you that you are not enough? That tell you what you can and cannot do? Will you look at the woman in the mirror and say, "I *can* do it. I am *worthy* of dreaming. And yes, I am *worthy* of something more!" Will you decide to be patient with yourself?

Know that we don't have to change everything at once. We can focus on tackling one small fear at a time and celebrate each win along the way. And as we conquer them, we'll start to feel it – freedom.

When we decide to let go of our fear and act on our dreams,

then all the focus on our own personal journey gains a deeper meaning as we begin to create our own fearless legacy. I often use the hashtag #betheexample and am *passionate* about it because whether we think so or not, people are watching – other women, other children, our own kids. And every day we have a choice whether or not to build them up, to lead by example, and to show what it means to let go of our fear and actually *live and dream.*

Even if we didn't have this positive example in our own lives, we can still *choose* to break the cycle of fear that is often passed from generation to generation. We have this amazing opportunity to change the tide, turn the ship, and take control. We have the power to say "I am worthy. I am *fearfully* made – *made to be respected and loved."* The power is in our hands. We just have to be truly honest, to look at ourselves in the mirror and ask ourselves some tough questions: Am I worth it? Am I willing to do the work? Am I willing to push through the "what ifs" and face the past? Am I willing to do it not only for me, but also for *them*?

We *can* break the cycle of fear. You were not respected? Then choose to respect. You haven't known forgiveness? Then *choose* to forgive. You weren't heard? Then choose to *listen.* You didn't feel loved? *Then choose to love. This* is how we become fearless and *this* is how we teach those who are watching us to live fearlessly.

All of us are called to greatness! For some of us it takes traveling a long road, filled with fear along the way, to even be able to grasp what greatness looks like and to recognize that yes, we are worthy of this greatness in our own lives. Then as we begin to let go of the fear, we find a glimmer of hope. We become more bold. We stretch the limits of our comfort zone, pushing that fear boundary further and further back, until we begin to feel it. Greatness.

Does this mean we'll no longer be afraid? No. Not at all. We'll always have fear, but that doesn't mean that we can't live a life of greatness and it doesn't mean that we can't live fearlessly. Living fearlessly is taking that step toward following our dream, approaching our fear boundary, feeling afraid and then walking through it *anyway*. It's knowing that the chains of feeling unlovable and unworthy are *gone*. It's knowing that we are *free* to follow our dreams, *free* to let go of our perfectionism and *free* to fail our way forward without worrying about the opinions of others.

Living fearlessly is about boldly saying "Yes we can!" It's making that daily choice to get back up when we fall, to face every day with courage and strength, and to believe that yes, we are worthy of greatness. It's about allowing ourselves to try new things, to accept each new challenge with grace, and to dream without limits.

And so I ask you again – Do you *dare* to dream? Are you ready to try something new? Are you willing to do the work to overcome your fear? To stop and ask yourself why you hesitate, name the root fear that's stopping you, claim it and then choose to walk forward boldly and overcome it?

My friend, it's time to stop thinking about doing something different and just *do* it. You were made for *more*, so I *dare* you to claim this! I *dare* you to let go of your fear. I *dare* you to allow yourself to dream. And I *dare* you to choose to live fearlessly!

AUTHOR'S NOTE

I've been talking about, teaching and reading about the topic of fear for the past few years. As with any topic close to our hearts, it's often hard to distinguish after a while where certain ideas came from. I had to ask myself during the writing of this book – Did this idea grow out of a conversation I had with a friend? A certain training or workshop I attended? A book I read? A podcast I listened to? A video I watched?

Below are some of the greatest influences that impacted my own development of this book, as I remember them. Any omissions from this list are unintentional and are mine alone.

My hope is that this list not only helps the reader to better understand the depth and complexity of the topic of fear and how it relates to so much of the world in which we live and learn and work, but that it inspires you to also use it as a list of suggested readings. My hope is that my book is only one of many that you read on your quest to becoming more fearless. I know now that it's possible.

Brene Brown, *Rising Strong*

Brene Brown, *The Power of Vulnerability*

Brene Brown, *Daring Greatly*

John C. Maxwell, *Failing Forward*

John C. Maxwell, *Intentional Living*

John C. Maxwell, *The 21 Irrefutable Laws of Leadership*

Napoleon Hill & W. Clement Stone, *Success Through a Positive Mental Attitude*

Dani Johnson, First Steps to Success Conference

Joyce Meyer, *The Battlefield of the Mind*

Holley Gerth, *You're Made for a God-Sized Dream*

Mark Batterson, *Draw The Circle, 40 Day Prayer Challenge*

Olivia Fox Cabane, *The Charisma Myth*

GRATITUDE

I have to start by thanking my family – my husband, Trent, and my six children, Joseph, Brigette, Nichole, Margarette, Jacqueline and Augustine. There is no way this book could have been written without your love and support and the many sacrifices you made along the way – the evenings you spent without me while I was digging into writing and editing this book, the extra chores you did, the meals made, laundry folded, the cups of coffee and meals brought to my desk – all of it. I love you more than I could ever express. You are my world. Thank you.

For my mom, Nancy, who taught me that I could do anything I put my mind to. Thank you for teaching me how to be resilient. And for my dad, Edward, for all those mornings you woke me up to go to church with you, helping to instill the faith that has brought me so much strength.

For my sisters, Dolly, Katie, Marianne, Eileen, Theresa, Jennifer, Rachael, Beth and Debbie. For being there for me, for allowing me to be there for you. For loving me through my intensity. For allowing me to learn from you. For making me feel lovable and worthy.

For my best friends, my sisters who have walked this journey with me. Who have held me when I cried. Who challenged me when I was wrong. Who loved me in spite of my many faults. Who reached out their hand to walk with me as I battled my fears. You know who you are. I am so grateful for you. I love you intensely.

For Kelley, my friend and success partner, who has been there every step of my own fear journey. For the many video calls and tears shed as we experienced growing pains as layer after layer of our walls came down and we learned how to be honest, how to get back up after failing, how to let go of the opinions of others and how to forgive. For walking with me as we worked together on changing our mindsets, learning how to communicate and choosing to live fearlessly and embrace freedom.

Thank you to Sommer for sharing so much of your heart as I began this journey. It is you who inspired me to pick up my first personal development book, take those first steps towards healing, to do *something different* and to live fearlessly. And to Rebekah for growing with me, believing in me, supporting me, and inviting me into your inner circle.

Thank you to the many women who opened their hearts to share their stories with me. This book and its message is much more powerful because of you. The tears shed and the laughter shared over our interviews were just the start of the ripple effect that has begun because you reached outside of yourselves to allow other women to learn and be inspired by your own stories of fear and fearlessness.

Thank you to Carrie, one of the women we featured in the last chapter of the book, for giving some of the very limited time she has left on Earth to share her heart and her life lessons in the hopes of making a difference. Carrie, you have *already* made a difference. Thank you! And thank you to her sister Jackie for connecting us and being there as we held the tear-driven, heartfelt interview.

For Erika, who throughout the writing of this book listened to me read for countless hours as chapter after chapter unfolded. For the advice you gave as we were finishing the book. Thank you for the feedback you provided, for your love, support and friendship.

Thank you to the many friends who spent countless hours giving feedback on book drafts, especially Erika, Tanner, Theresa, Belinda, Lauren, Alison, Megan, Kate, Anita, and Carrie. For my sister Katie who took the time to listen to me share about the book and helped solidify some of my ideas. Thank you for taking the time out of your busy lives to help improve this book and make it stronger.

Thank you to the Piano Guys for your version of the song

"A Thousand Years" which I listened to on repeat and which brought me so much inspiration throughout the writing of this book.

Thanks to the entire team at Full Circle Press who helped bring my dream of writing this book to life. From design and layout to editing and publishing, you all have helped me produce something of which I am very proud. Thanks to Laura for being so patient with me as we worked to get the design and layout just right. And a special thanks to Marina, who coached me and worked alongside me the entire way. You helped to solidify many of my thoughts and concepts, lent your interviewing, writing and editing expertise, and put so much of your heart and time into this project. I'm so grateful for the countless hours you sacrificed to help make this dream a reality. You pushed me far beyond where I was comfortable and have been a catalyst for a lot of personal growth over the last year. Thank you for taking this journey with me, for being so patient, and for believing in me the whole way through.

And finally, for all those who believed in me when I struggled to believe in myself. Thank you.

ABOUT THE AUTHOR

Michelle Hillaert is a work-at-home mom who is passionate about writing and sharing her message of living fearlessly. With a degree in Communication Arts, Michelle has been everything from a computer technician to a website and image designer to a social media manager. She is currently a Network Marketing professional and leads a growing team of health and fitness coaches. Wife to Trent and mother to six beautiful children, Michelle is dedicated to her family, active in her community, and loves to volunteer.

If you enjoyed Let Go of the Fear, you can find additional resources at www.LetGooftheFear.com and www.michellehillaert.com

You can also connect with Michelle in the following ways:

Blog: www.MichelleHillaert.com

Facebook: www.Facebook.com/MichelleHillaertFit

Instagram: @mhillaert

Twitter: @mhillaert

ABOUT FULL CIRCLE PRESS

Full Circle Press is a socially-conscious, purpose-driven independent publishing house with a deep commitment to contributing to the greater good through helping to write, edit, publish and market books that matter. We believe in changing the world one story at a time and we envision a world where quality books and literacy resources are available to all. We are educators at heart and are passionate about teaching what we know, sharing resources when and where we can, and empowering others to do and be better. Visit www.fullcirclepress.org to learn more about our products, programs, and services.